SUNDIAL
IN
ANGEL SQUARE

A
SUNDIAL
IN
ANGEL SQUARE

A Memoir

John S. Foley

Woodside Publications

Copyright © John S. Foley

ISBN 0 9521739 0 5   A SUNDIAL IN ANGEL SQUARE

British Library Cataloguing-in-Publication Data.
A catalogue record for this book is available from the British Library.

First published 1993 by Woodside Publications,
"Woodside", Harman's Cross, Corfe Castle,
Wareham, Dorset BH20 5HY
Tel: 01929 480676

Second edition 1994
Third edition 1996
Reprinted 1998

Cover illustration by Lawrence Littleton Evans

smallprint
typesetting & printing
35 Silver Birches Haywards Heath West Sussex RH16 3PD
Telephone 01444 457101

Acknowledgment

A foreword is unnecessary because the reader should very quickly grasp the writer's objective, but acknowledgment must be made for valuable help received prior to printing. For this I must mention my dear friend Keith Weber, who before being approached about this was unknown to me, and who since then has laboured to understand my writing and also my thinking before getting those thoughts into context. As we got to know each other he found himself free to suggest that motor trade 'jargon' was not suitable for all readers, and expressed concern about my expression "dirty trick" when used in connection with an incident initiated by my beloved father! Of course, that was how an eleven-year-old felt when it happened, but it had to be re-phrased before printing. Others who have heard my story on tape have made helpful suggestions.

However, behind all that is presented within these covers is a prayer that positive help may be received by any who, like the writer, desire a closer walk with God in everyday living.

Foreword

This latest reprint is evidence of the large number of copies which have found their way into people's homes and hopefully have been read.

There are many reasons for writing a memoir, but the intentions of this writer are clear from the outset: in exposing his own life and experience to public view he really wants his readers to look above and beyond, from the author of this book to the Author of life. For those whose perspective is thus changed this book will have served its purpose.

KW, April 1998

*To my four daughters, still with me,
who, with their beloved mother,
gave loving support throughout.*

Contents

	Page
Acknowledgment	v
Introduction	1
1: Adjusting the Timing	3
2: The Foley Brothers	8
3: Foley Junior	20
4: Formative Experiences in a Christian Home	29
5: Into the Fray	46
6: A New Enterprise	57
7: Tools of the Trade	71
8: Under the Counter	80
9: Over the Counter	90
10: Regular Service	114
11: Hymns	122
12: Under Instruction	132
13: Business As Usual	146
Postscript	151

Illustrations:

"So Speed We But The Reckoning Bideth"	5
Family photo at Layton	7
Group outside typical meeting hut	12
Interior of meeting hut	13
Uncle and Father — tricycle and bicycle	17
Slepe Cottage in early 1900s	20
Slepe Cottage in 1960s	21
Postcard of Shaftesbury, 1907	23
This 'Oil Rag'!	53
Author with Triumph Seven Fabric Saloon	56
Author and wife on wedding day	58
Family photo	60
First page of "The Traveller's Guide"	62
Foley's Garage (as it was)	67
Aunt Annie	97
Author with two mechanics	146
Opening of the new premises	148
The Author	Back cover

Poems and Hymns: *Page*

The Finding	41
Love's Infinitude	43
The Quest	74
The Christian Workshop	79
Safely Anchored	90
The Sower	93
On Diet	104
The Two Prayers	107
Loyalty	110
Episcopy	113
Caesarea Philippi	122
I Love the Lord	123
The New Birth	124
The New Look	125
At Home	126
My Shepherd	127
New Things	128
The Easy Yoke	129
Transcendency	130
Why the Cross?	131
Fruit of the Spirit	135
The Seeker	155

Introduction

This is the tale of a Christian who has spent over sixty-five years in the Motor Trade, and much of my story has to be told from that perspective.

Until I became an octogenarian nothing was further from my thoughts than to write a memoir; but, with the passage of time affecting the memory, the truth has dawned that the finishing-post must be getting near, and an incident which occurred some six decades ago now drives me on with a sense of urgency to write this account.

I refer to a talk given to a company of young people, of whom I was one, in Norwich Avenue Chapel, Bournemouth. All I can recall is the text, and particularly the question oft repeated by the speaker. The text runs: "We spend our years as a tale that is told" (Psalm 90:9 in the Authorised Version of the Bible); while the question he pressed with some vigour ran: "Will *yours* be a tale worth telling?"

No doubt the speaker was well aware that many miss their way in life, reaching the end with little to record which would be of help to someone in search of peace. Such is the thought conveyed by alternative translations of this same verse. For example: "We finish our years with a moan" (New International Version); "Our years come to an end like a sigh" (Revised Standard Version); "Our years die away like a murmur" (New English Bible).

Sombre reading indeed! But the context in which these words are found makes for profitable study, as the hymn writer Isaac Watts appears to have done in giving us "O God, our help in ages past, our hope for years to come".

Many men and women have had tales to tell from their lives; but it is the writer's conviction that, in the final analysis, there is no life record really worth the telling unless that life is one committed to Jesus Christ.

When Psalms 90 and 91 are taken together, we are brought face to face with God who is to be trusted to see us through to the finish. It is my prayer that He will use my tale in helping someone who, like the writer, is ever in need of Someone bigger than himself.

This is the original cover illustration, which relates to the incident described at the top of page 6.

1: Adjusting the Timing

While this is going to be a record of the love and unfailing grace of God our Father in His handling of a difficult child (!), it must not be thought that the writer has known little of victory. Many lessons were learnt the hard way, it is true; but learnt they were, and he does know where he has come from and where he is going; and this, I repeat, is all by the grace of God.

It is a mistake to think that the Christian life must be dull; to live under the authority of God and seek His guidance is an exciting adventure, full of surprises, and as I tell of childhood, school, employment, home and business life, together with church activities, I trust a picture will emerge in which God's hand is unmistakably clear. Satan will be referred to as a real person, the great enemy of God and man who has ever been seeking to impose his will on me. The period covered by my story will begin some ten years before my birth, and so my forebears will be given some prominence. Many have made an impact on my life, not least my family. This is a story of God running after me and using many in the process; some are with us today, and how loyal they are!

Alternative uses of my name will be noted. This arose because the name given me was John, the same as my uncle's, with whom father worked closely. To mother I would always be "John", or something endearing. Father would use "Son" on occasions, and this would usually be accompanied by some advice or encouragement; but never did he use his brother's name on me. More often it would be "Jack", the name leaving his lips like the backfire of a car! My friends in the motor trade insisted on "Jack", and my reader is invited to do likewise.

Still on the subject of names, visiting an old friend, Sergeant Towndrow, early in our married life, I was given a welcome that caught my breath. The door was opened by a pleasantly surprised little man who seemed able to lay hold of a verse for every occasion: "A man sent from God whose name was John ... Come in, thou blessed of the Lord!" With hindsight, I should have told him to 'hold it', because John the Baptist said of Jesus, "He must increase but I must decrease" — a self-abnegation it is taking me a lifetime to learn! However, I appreciated his warmth, and a word about my friend will be of interest.

Converted while serving in India, and later engaged as an Army Scripture Reader, his preaching certainly held attention. I remember his happy face looking over the top of the reading desk and misquoting the text to make his point! "He is able to save to the 'guttermost' them that come unto God by Him." Of course, he would have enlarged on the fact that not all find themselves in the gutter as he had done, but the Lord blessed his testimony.

So much for the present on my name; I shall be referring to three Johns later in my story, all very different.

Taking a lady whose car was in for service back to her home one day, the chat must have drifted somewhat from the job in hand, because she left me with: "I don't want God to control my life, thank you!" I must have got the 'timing' wrong because we never saw her again!

The reader is asked to accept mixed metaphors; the apostle Paul did this at times and it will be noted that he is held by the writer in high esteem. I am also hoping the reason for my jumping about 'timewise' will be made clear by the context. It all has to do with God's controlling hand upon my life.

When at school, I was never adept in keeping the ball close to my foot; nor could I see the need to pass it to someone better placed: after all, the idea was to get it in yonder goal! It was not only the sports master who had problems: if the window was open when my class was in session it would be my name the locals would hear — *"Foley, pay attention!"* Of course, good teachers have no

Adjusting the Timing

need to shout, but as I look back I thank God for His goodness in raising His voice in order to secure my attention. This will appear as my story unfolds, together with His quieter voice speaking to my conscience, in particular concerning the reckoning day ahead. It is this thought that settles the title for my tale and provides the reason for bringing in so much about my forebears, as this has an important bearing on that early part of my training.

And so to the title given to this memoir. We now jump to the age of twelve. Cycling down the High Street into Angel Square on my way to school, I would pass one of Shaftesbury's old relics: a sundial set high in the wall, and with this inscription:

SO SPEED WE BUT THE RECKONING BIDETH

A little further, the photographer's shop carried this one in bold letters:

SECURE THE SHADOW ERE THE SUBSTANCE FADETH

Quite arresting for any that would pause to read, as both call to mind that Time, with its opportunity, is passing; so too are youth and beauty. Taken together they are saying, "Get moving, but watch your step!"

"So Speed We But The Reckoning Bideth"

A SUNDIAL IN ANGEL SQUARE

I was moving quite fast along this particular route on one such occasion, pedalling hard as I rounded the bend by the square, completely unaware of the pack of hounds, followed by huntsmen, approaching from the opposite direction! I certainly heard no 'winding of the horn', or even a dog bark, but within seconds I provided onlookers with a sight and sound to be remembered beneath that sundial! I had often heard those animals during feeding time, the kennels being only a mile from home, but I had never witnessed a 'kill'!

The master of the hunt was more concerned about my wellbeing than the fate of his hounds. However, amidst the confusion of bicycle, boy and barking beagles I was unhurt, though I could not answer for the dogs! I was in "Angel Square"! — and this brings me to speak of a picture I still hold from childhood.

Two small children, hand in hand, are walking on the edge of a cliff. One is trying to catch a butterfly, and just in front of them the path has given way. Overshadowing them is an angel with outstretched wings and hands. Is this an example of Victorian sentimentality, or is it the sentiment expressed in Psalm 91:11?

Cycling home from school would involve negotiating Nettlebed Corner, a dangerous bend near the bottom of the hill, and not far from home. (At least two soldiers on bicycles were killed on this corner during the first World War.) To take it without touching the brake required practice, and it could be done if there was a head wind! But to stop at our cottage a brake was essential and if *it* was not working your foot served the purpose.

Father effectively put a stop to this technique one day by suddenly appearing at the gate: "Did I hear you drag your foot on the ground to stop?" Then, without waiting for the lie, he tried the brake! I knew it was useless to tell him about shining angels — his mind was on my safety and the price of shoe leather!

My home life was strict, but not unhappy, and in giving

Adjusting the Timing

my experience I am helped by a number of photos; but I regret the loss of Mother's Bible in which she recorded the date when I asked Jesus to save me. This happened when I was eight, following her reading to me of "Christie's Old Organ", and would be of particular interest to me because, some time later in a fit of temper, I crossed it out — then repented and wrote it in again!

Shortly after I had come to Jesus for salvation, Grandma asked me in Uncle's presence,

"Have you told Uncle that you have now been saved?"

"Oh ... Uncle, I have now been saved."

"Oh yes? Glad to hear that. Who saved you?" he replied mischievously.

"Mummy."

It was left to Grandma to clarify the situation!

Aunt Annie   Father   Mother
Uncle John   Grandma   Uncle Albert   Friend
Ruth   John
(Taken during the First World War)

2: The Foley Brothers

I want now to speak about my beloved parents long before I arrived, because my history is bound up very largely with theirs.

Fredrick Foley, the youngest of five children, was born at Seaford in the year 1874, and completed his education at Seaford College. His father, Charles Foley, was employed in H.M. Customs at Newhaven. From there, the family moved to Southampton, Liverpool, Edinburgh, and finally to Bristol, where Charles Foley died.

It was in Edinburgh at the age of nineteen that Fred came to know the Lord Jesus as a personal Saviour — John 5:24 being the verse that brought him assurance: "Verily, verily, I say unto you, He that heareth my word, and believeth on him that sent me, hath everlasting life, and shall not come into condemnation; but is passed from death unto life."

Fred found employment in the watches and clocks department in Jenners of Princes Street. It was there he met Margaret Scott who worked in the glass and chinaware side of the store. (I shall refer to other members of the Scott family in due course and shall find joy in so doing.) Father tells the story of someone setting all the alarm clocks to go off when the manager was there alone! The sequel was somewhat garbled, but the undisputed facts were these: Fred was already on the point of leaving Edinburgh and had spent his holiday with his older brother who had for some time been working as an evangelist in Dorset and who was at that time working with caravan and tent in the village of Puddletown; while there John persuaded him to hand in his notice and join him in full-time service for the Lord.

By this time the family had moved to Bristol — which probably had something to do with Fred's seeking to move south. Margaret, fully prepared to marry a man with no salary (and no church or society behind him),

The Foley Brothers

came to Bristol where they were united in marriage. The service was conducted in Bethesda Chapel, Bristol, by Dr Fred Bergin of the Ashleydown Orphanage; and it was in Bristol that occasionally they were privileged to sit under the ministry of George Müller, the founder of that institution.

This is interesting because I have no doubt that Müller's views on baptism, and a ministry that carried no fixed salary, very largely influenced Father's thinking. This will offer explanation for the manner of life he was to follow; taking with him a wife who was one with him in this respect. In fact, Margaret had to return to Edinburgh for a while shortly after the marriage until a cottage became available for them in Sturminster Newton.

In stepping out in full dependence on the Lord for the needed financial support, the Foley brothers were by no means alone; numbers were increasing who had seen a New Testament pattern of life that the Lord would honour. They were aware that it would entail hardship, and at times their faith would be tested, that it "might be found unto praise and honour and glory at the appearing of Jesus Christ" (1 Peter 1:7).

To choose the Ministry as a career without having experienced the New Birth is hard to understand, but it happens, and a case comes to mind. I once found courage to ask a minister, who spent many of his holidays in Purbeck, if he came to know the Lord before ordination or after. His reply was revealing: he said, "I was a priest for over fourteen years before I was saved!" I would judge his preaching changed radically when the miracle took place. Certainly his message was with great power when on several occasions he spoke at the Gospel Hall.

Whilst I do not recall ever putting the question to Father, I have no doubt he firmly believed God called him to preach the gospel. However, I have often queried in mind if he ever received encouragement, apart from his brother, to go into full-time service as an evangelist;

because, though he had many gifts, preaching was not one of them. Had it been, much of the help given to younger men might have been lost; as it was, those under his care found him to be a great encourager. Realising his own limitations in this field, he had keen insight into their potential and encouraged them in the exercise of their developing gifts.

This reminds me of an incident during a recent meeting of Trustees, when a member who was widely thought of as a speaker with some gift remarked with disapproval on "tight-lipped" brothers present at a meeting for worship he had attended at that chapel — referring to the long silences during the service, apparently because the men seemed reluctant to contribute verbally. His complaint received an immediate response from one of the offenders: "That's because you were there, brother!" Though spoken in lighter vein, this reply had its point, for the speaker had been held somewhat in awe by the others, and their estimation of his gift in comparison with their abilities had caused them to hold themselves in check.

With Father, however, this problem did not arise. Much of his life was given to guiding young men who had heard God's call to preach the gospel and had been commended for this work by various churches that shared their vision and would support them. He took the view that if these men were depending on *fellow Christians* meeting their financial needs, they would have much to learn! On the other hand, if they were trusting *the Lord* to use whatever means He willed to supply their need, they would still have much to learn, but it would be more of their Lord who had called them to a pathway of faith.

Father, through his wide reading, was a tremendous help to Uncle, who was very gifted as a preacher. His beaming smile enhanced the Good News that he was proclaiming; but, not being a Bible student, he leaned heavily on his brother who was able to dig deep into God's Word.

The Foley Brothers

The Foley brothers rejected the teaching of J. N. Darby and others of a 'secret rapture' of the church before the time of tribulation, which was finding wide acceptance in their circle of fellowship at that time, following rather the traditional view held by B. W. Newton, G. Müller, S. P. Tregelles, R. Chapman, Dan Crawford, and many others. Consequently a certain amount of tension prevailed. In later years, however, all this disappeared, both pre- and post-tribulation camps being of one mind that the coming of the Lord for His people is the vital incentive to holiness of life — a message to be preached loud and clear with the Lord's blessing. It will interest some of my readers to know that their mother followed 'Mr Darby' very closely on the subject, and this lovely woman will appear again in my story, as will also her counterpart, Grandma Scott.

At that time Theological Colleges, or Bible Schools, were held to be somewhat out of line with the position held by Brethren churches and in some quarters were frowned upon as a departure from New Testament teaching. Young men who had given up their jobs, stepping out in faith into full-time service for the Lord, needed training, however, and Father went some way to meeting that need, spending time in Bible study with them and helping them prepare for their work in other ways, beside the proclamation of the gospel message. While at the time of writing, when extraordinary changes are taking place worldwide and especially in Europe, colleges which are evangelical in outlook are full to capacity.

But to return to the newly married, a cottage was found on the Common at Sturminster Newton with the bare necessities that would make it a home; and a year later they moved to Hazelbury Bryan where my sister Ruth was born. I could list six Dorset villages where they lived before I arrived, all in five years!

It was a simple life, full of variety because quite often they would have young men staying with them for a while, sharing their plain fare, all in preparation for serving the Lord at home or abroad. Mother was good at making a splendid dish out of little and at no time did they go hungry; it was no different in my day — they lived on the same level as the people they sought to win for the Lord.

A word now about how the Foley brothers worked. We have spoken of their status, from which it will be understood that no collections were taken at their meetings, not even a box for expenses at the door. (I hasten to add that Father bent on that point later when a young church was being established.)

Group outside hut. Father and Mother (holding Ruth) and Uncle are on extreme right of picture. Dated 1906.

A canvas tent, or a hut in the winter months, each holding about thirty-plus, would be assembled if possible in time for the children to advertise a meeting in the evening. Sankey's hymns would be led by Uncle on the harmonium, or perhaps by Father using a 'squeeze box'; both could sing well. The choruses used would be words of Scripture, usually. Uncle's preaching held the attention

The Foley Brothers

Interior of hut, with Father and Uncle.

of all ages and, although I was quite young, a sample comes to mind. Stories from *Daniel* had been given with aids for the memory — "Now, children, how do we remember the names of the three men that were thrown into the fiery furnace?" — then a chorus of voices, "Shake the bed, make the bed, and into bed he goes!" The children would remember that one as I did and would not be left thinking it was a fairy tale. They would not only remember the names Shadrach, Meshach and Abednego, but they would find a name for the fourth person that joined those brave men.

When speaking of man's responsibility to respond to God's mercy and the urgency of the message, no lightness whatever was used, nor was there any 'back-pedalling' on the subject of eternal punishment of the wicked if they do not repent, often referred to by the Lord Jesus. In the end it was the love of God that won and *John 3:16* would be quoted on almost every occasion; indeed, a verse to be learned by heart before they left the village.

In seeking to help young men in preaching the gospel, both evangelists stressed the importance of the public reading of Scripture. The Bible should be read in a manner that will not only command the listener's attention, but will commend itself as the Word of God. Otherwise, the urgency, power and comfort will be lost through lack of clarity. Some gifted expositors seem to forget that not all can run so fast, and appear to be reading solely to jog their own memory! Surely it should be read in such a way that both reader and listener are conscious that God is speaking.

This leads me to a question that is causing some concern to many Christians today, and one that was not so apparent in the early days, although I remember some declamation when speakers used the Revised Version of 1888. More recently, I was asked if I had ever heard of anyone being saved through reading that version! The view of my questioner is still held by many; some going so far as to place a note on the reading desk requesting that the King James' Version provided should be used! In meeting this request, the writer has felt the rather naughty urge to say he will be reading from the Revised Version of 1611!

Language changes with time, but God's truth will stand firm for every age. Personally, my quotation of Scripture has to be that which was memorised as a child, and this will be reflected in this memoir; but I am sure the wide range of sound versions to hand has provided me with a God-given advantage over my forebears, as my car does over their bicycles! I am still left with a problem, however, because I can see that the congregation should be encouraged to follow the reading (and perhaps participate). This opens the question: what version shall we provide? — and the difficulty remains.

In Father's day no impact had been made to control the

minds by radio or television; also, away from the towns, there were no places of entertainment; and so, generally speaking, hearts were more open to hear the good news of the gospel, often with a real thirst for spiritual help. Such conditions account for the considerable amount of help given to the brothers in transporting equipment, or moving home from village to village, or from site to site. Police or publican, farmer or farm-hand — all seemed to combine in helping rather than frustrating their activities. That, of course, is not all the story! Some clergy who were very disturbed about what they saw as an intrusion into their parish, having been visited by one of the brothers before setting up their tent, discouraged some people from attending. There were others, though, who were in full sympathy and glad that these visitors had the courage to give a clear message, and no doubt got a real blessing themselves.

In contrast to the present day, when time and motion study seems to be a part of life, we can see that then there was more time to think, read and pray — and also to listen! A cycle journey of several miles would give time for meditation before a meeting, which would often take place in a cottage packed with neighbours, the village having previously been visited with the tent. This reminds me of an incident when staying with an evangelist friend of mine in Oxfordshire, William Mitchell by name. We called at the house of someone he had not seen for several years, and the door was opened by this lady who, with a shout, rushed forward to embrace him, saying, "I thank God every day of my life that He ever sent you to our village to get me saved!"

Whilst great earnestness marked their preaching, the Foley brothers avoided using high pressure, or what they termed "pulling in the net", methods for getting decisions. It was left to the Holy Spirit to do His work in His own way.

About the time I joined the family circle interest was

growing in the brothers' activities by Brethren churches in Dorset, and young men were encouraged to cycle out and help in the meetings; many have looked back on those opportunities with gratitude. Their attention would doubtless be drawn to the finer points of wisdom — "Be yourself, don't ape someone else!", or concerning eating habits and other such matters! It would not be out of place to say that both Father and Uncle could see the funny side to a situation, and perhaps some of this has rubbed off on the writer!

I am fully aware that Satan can use frivolity to advantage, but I do thank God that I am able to enjoy a laugh whilst walking close to Him. I can bang away on the piano and sing with the children:

> All that I am He made me,
> All that I have He gave me,
> All that I ever hope to be
> Jesus alone must do for me.
>   (C.S.S.M. Choruses).

Life for some people is a huge joke and it is not easy to talk seriously. I worked for years with one of that make-up and later, when I started on my own, he came to work for me. George was a likable fellow, though not a Christian, and he would tone down the content if I were about! He once told me that Christians were not supposed to laugh! He paid dear for his exuberance, however, and required re-stitching after an operation! As a lad this man had attended the meetings for children when Father was working in Langton Matravers and he would sing the choruses where he was apprenticed, much to the annoyance of his foreman. In fact, this nearly cost him his job because neither the boss nor the foreman wanted to hear "The best book to read is the Bible" — and the latter was determined the nuisance should cease! A heavy hammer, thrown from a distance and striking his work bench, did the job effectively!

Much prayer had been made for George, and a friend

told me that he found tears of repentance before he died.

In a photo before me, I see my uncle pushing a heavily loaded tricycle, with Father doing the same on two wheels. They look smart in breeches and stockings but I am assured these carry no ecclesiastical status! Later, a single-cylinder De Dion car with no hood was used; and as a four-year-old I remember yelling my disgust at having to walk up a hill near Bristol (the car wouldn't have made it otherwise) while Father waited for us at the top!

Uncle and Father — tricycle and bicycle.

Although working together, Uncle (who never married) seldom lived under the same roof as Father. He used a large caravan that would stand beside the marquee; and a word now about its inglorious end. It was a huge, and therefore heavy, affair on four wheels, and requiring the same number of horses to pull it. I remember seeing its last journey to Langton Matravers via Kingston Hill (there was no valley road in those days) and feeling very unhappy about the use of the whip — a kind of fellow feeling, I guess!

One night some months later a south-west gale, taking advantage of its exposed position, did a perfect job, with Uncle suddenly finding himself in the open air amid a pile of timber and, in the mercy of God, unhurt. He told us he was glad he let the fire out because he found himself embracing the 'black demon' (the coke stove which would glow red-hot when alight)!

As we consider members of my family long since passed to their rest, it will be noted that their simple faith held without question (without question — but not blindly) to God's Word, which says, "All things work together for good to them that love God, to them that are called according to His purpose" (Romans 8:28).

Following a fall in the street when living in Poole, my Grandma was heard to say, as she was being carried to her bed in the arms of my Uncle, "This is one of the 'all things', John." This testimony from her lips revealed that she was one of those who loved God and had come to know Him as Father; a relationship that had begun long before when she took her place before Him needing mercy, placing her faith in Jesus. For the mouth speaks according to what is in the heart (see Matthew 12:33-37).

It needs to be emphasised that all movement in our hearts towards God begins with God, the vital link being faith. Faith is God's way for man first to enter His fold and it is by faith man then lives within that fold.

I have often heard people speak in these terms: "I'd give anything to have your faith" (though they don't usually mean it!); or: "I wish I had your faith, it all sounds so simple, but I haven't got it." I sometimes wonder if the person who says he wants faith is in real earnest about the matter, because I have been surprised at the apparent resistance of some to read their Bible in order to examine the claims of Jesus, who said: "I and my Father are one" (John 10:30).

Who is this that claims equality with God? Is he all that he claims to be? What is the evidence on which faith must rest? As Jesus himself said: "If anyone chooses to do God's will, he will find out whether my teaching comes from God or whether I speak on my own" (John 7:17).

If the one who is seeking has come thus far he will find himself face to face with the death and resurrection of Jesus; and, before I proceed, a Scripture comes to mind that leads me again to say that faith is vital: "... without faith it is impossible to please Him: for he that comes to God must believe that He is, and that He is a rewarder of them that diligently seek Him" (Hebrews 11:6).

So, if a person desires faith because he has a conscience that is troubling him, he is on the right lines in his seeking, because conviction of sin is the work of the Holy Spirit (John 16:8). He is leading this man to repent, to acknowledge his sin and look to the living Christ who died on the cross. In this way, the Christian loses all hope in himself and leans his whole weight on Jesus, who is now his Lord. This is the faith we are talking about in this memoir.

Some twenty years after the Foley brothers left the Blackmoor Vale for South Dorset, Stanley Wilcox was covering the same villages with the gospel and using similar methods. But by this time the wireless was beginning to offer counter attractions. Whilst this is still true today, radio and television are nevertheless being used to beam the gospel worldwide.

3: Foley Junior

Before I tell of my birth and its setting, I will deal with a point that may arise in the mind of my reader — indeed, I ask myself the question: Is anyone going to find help through 'looking at my washing as it hangs on the line'? My prayer is that he might be led to focus his eye on the wide vista above my line and come to the same conclusion as another John, who gave us the hymn based on his own experience, but using a different metaphor:

> *Amazing grace, how sweet the sound*
> *That saved a wretch like me.*
>
> (John Newton)

Slepe Cottage in the early 1900s.

Slepe Cottage is now an attractive Café and Guest House near Lychett Minster, and it was there that my life began on February 7th, 1909. I find the name interesting because my parents always referred to my birthplace as 'Slip'; but I have before me a cutting taken from a local paper dated 1968 with a picture of the cottage, under which are the following words:

Slepe Cottage more recently.

"Slepe is a small place on the road to Dorchester beyond the Bakers' Arms. In the old days the Saxons found this undrained hinterland of Poole Harbour a miry place, and so the place-name was born. The word derives from the Old English word 'slaep', which an authority on place names says 'is usually held to mean a slippery or miry place'."

No doubt my reader will remember that word as I proceed! Each time I pass this notable spot I have a vision of my Father going all out on his bicycle into Poole for the doctor, and then beating him to it for the event! More about that later; for the moment I am thinking of Mother — the best mother in the world!

The weekly shopping trip with pram and five-year-old red-headed girl meant a journey of five miles each way into Wareham and, as some old photos reveal, voluminously attired for the dusty trek. I am told that whilst in a café this small boy swallowed a farthing that he found in the handbag and the doctor would not allow them to return until it was recovered!

From Slepe we moved to Cheddar. Why this move to Somerset for three years or so is lost, but that is where my memory begins. Apparently (I am told) the baptistry in the Gospel Hall was being filled and this small boy asked his Uncle what it was for. Father would have been more careful in his reply, but not Uncle: "That is where people that love the Lord Jesus are put!" I doubt if I gave him the opportunity to explain that this would only be at the request of these people. There are many adults that feel the same as I did then, when facing baptism by immersion!

When World War I broke out we were living at Nailsea (west of Bristol), and I recall my sister, now aged ten, explaining what men do in war! Very interesting to this small boy, but on no account was *he* given guns or the like to play with. Although Father was a 'conscientious objector', he felt his place should be amongst the troops back in Dorset; and it was on Blandford Camp that he and his brother stayed throughout the war. I shall refer to them again in this context.

Considerable space will be given to my childhood because I am sure it was the most important part of my eighty years. Shaftesbury is the town where my story really begins, and it will be noted as I proceed that, up to my 'teen age, Father doesn't appear often. His call to preach the gospel involved adjustment to family life, and this was foreseen and accepted over the years. When at school, we would see him about one day in two weeks, but never on a Sunday, except when I stayed with him in the caravan, which were good days for me and made up for the occasions when his hard and horny hand had to do its job in discipline when at home!

In the years that followed I never lost respect for my dear father, as I trust my tale will make clear.

Furthermore, my sister Ruth and I saw little of each other in my school years; but I shall refer to her again.

Hanging in my lounge is a large picture of Shaftesbury that catches my eye every day, reviving memories, both good and otherwise! It was painted at my request by my sister-in-law, Adele Cleall, being taken from a post-card that Mother received several years before I was born, and shows Layton House standing in the foreground. Little did Mother think that nine years later she would be living in one part of that building.

Post-card showing Shaftesbury in 1907. Layton House is just right of centre.

It was a rambling house with many bedrooms where, in the early days of the First World War, twelve soldiers were billeted for a while. By that time Father's family had left Bristol and so a lot of Foleys were living under the same roof, the entrance hall dividing the two families: Grandma Foley, Aunt Annie and Uncle John on one side; Father, Mother, Ruth and I on the other.

Grandma's side of the house was full of good Victorian furniture, and so in no way was I given the run of the house; but with the large garden and croquet lawn, also a coach house in which was stored that old De Dion car, I was not at a loss in looking for mischief! I see the large Tulip tree standing on the lawn; also the Walnut tree in our three-acre field that made me popular with the lads. I see (or I think I do) the old Mulberry tree whose leaves fed my silk-worms. On the end of the house is my bedroom that had a sloping floor that made you feel queer. I did quite a bit of scheming as well as sleeping in that room. But then I also see the window of the little sitting room where Mother read 'Christie's Old Organ' to me, and when something took place in my wicked little heart and never left. Indeed, all the rooms I can see remind me of some kind of confrontation, and also some marvellous escapades!

On occasions, a well-behaved little boy was allowed to cross the hall and enjoy a lovely tea. Mother had done her job well and I even drank the China tea without a murmur; her problem began when I returned. Living so close to her 'in-laws', life was not easy for Mother at times. Missionaries tell us about their need for patience when living in close contact with their fellow workers without a break for three or four years. Nevertheless, I know that Mother often found comfort by seeking it across the hall.

The problems my sister Ruth gave were largely due to ill health, and she was boarded at the Park School, Yeovil. When we all left Layton House in 1921, Ruth also went with her Grandma to Poole. Prior to World War II she went to Morocco to teach English and after the fall of France we heard nothing of her for three years until she phoned from Southampton, having been flown to Stoney

Cross Air Strip by the R.A.F. Ruth never returned to North Africa although her heart was there, and, whatever views she had concerning God's purpose for the Jewish nation, it was a pro-Arab sister that came home, leaving many close friends behind!

Her parents had been told when she was a child that she was unlikely to reach the age of twenty. She was, however, able to give devoted attention to Mother, and later to Father, until she died at the age of fifty-five. The problem of those early days no longer existed; and in the months before she died we got much closer to each other. When taking her for a drive through the Dorset villages she knew so well she told me her only grief was that she was not going to see Father through to the end of his life ... he in fact survived her by nine years.

Moving from Layton House to Rock Cottage, Enmore Green, on the other side of Shaftesbury, life for both Mother and I was to undergo some change and we were going to get to know each other in a different way. She would now find herself very much alone; it was a time of adjustment for us both in more ways than one.

The cottage itself was very small, with no gas or water laid on. All the cooking was done on a three-burner Valor Perfection oil stove that really did a good job in pushing out heat and smell! One little matter that our occasional visitors found somewhat trying was the 'privy' being situated half way up the garden with its door facing the road!

Before I left for school, it was my job each morning to fetch a day's supply of water from a pump some distance up the hill. So the old bicycle (my sister's cast-off!) is now seen to be fulfilling a useful role. The precious commodity is carried in a large watering can on the handlebars; care was required if a second trip was to be avoided.

The cottage lay hard on the main road with its narrow garden running with it, and on the end of which was a large text placed there by the previous owner — and it was part of the sale agreement that it remained. It read: PREPARE TO MEET THY GOD. Father, who was seldom at home, was not averse to keeping this arresting message in its prominent position — though perhaps a more suitable place would have been up the road, just before Nettlebed corner!

Mother, however, found that every hungry tramp thought this would be the place where his tin could be replenished! None was ever turned away. This and tract distribution were Mother's work for the Lord, and, although attended with much fear and trembling, there was also much joy. I have heard Father speak of this service as lacking limelight, but not delight. Like him, Mother was not gifted for speaking in meetings, but her approach in offering a Gospel booklet had a sweetness that few could resist. She would never sing a solo before a company, but passers-by would hear her lovely voice singing, "What a Friend we have in Jesus" as she moved about the house.

A word more about that lady's bicycle — my pride and joy, loaded with various items collected from the dump, ingeniously attached. Ignorant people just looked and laughed; but this wonderful machine carried me on my holidays to Poole and back, thirty miles each way, and grand holidays they were, too — helping with the boats in the park, bathing at Sandbanks with company like-minded, and connected with Mount Street Gospel Hall. They were days to be remembered. I never had any money and so never missed it. A recent speaker at Woodside Chapel, Harold Foster, reminded me of the fate of that bicycle. Riding hard down the High Street with Harold sitting frontways on the handlebars, I was suddenly conscious that he was gradually coming onto my lap; so much so that we both ended up on the road! The frame had done a superb job for three years but had never been asked to perform that act and buckled under the weight! How I returned to Shaftesbury, or what explanation I offered, I do not recall; no doubt it would be rust that was to blame, for truth was not always my strong point!

This may provide old employees with some light as to why they received a lecture on truthfulness when they approached me in search of work, human nature being what it is. Mother's warning concerning the fate of liars (based on her understanding of Revelation 21:8) ensured my being very unhappy if I resorted to 'terminological inexactitudes', and I wished to save them that!

Now that Father had graduated to a motorcycle, and I to his old machine, life was getting very interesting; I was catching up with him. The most sensible thing that Father ever did was to give up that mode of travel; the last being a four-valve, four-speed Rudge with a huge sidecar. It was quite a thing in its day and, with Father on the saddle, was normally ridden flat out! Mother seldom braved that sidecar, and I never: my seat was on the pillion where I could jump off if occasion demanded. As soon as I was given a licence, I was able to give Father a dose of his own medicine — how foolish we can be!

I bring these details into my story to show my readers that the bias in my nature was inherited. My beloved parents were very conscious of this and were often on their knees about it, as I discovered in later years.

With the birth of our first child, I was given wisdom to give up that means of transport, moving to a Morgan three-wheeler, and from there to the comparative safety of an old Morris Cowley. This was an open tourer that I bought for £5 because it had a broken chassis. This wonderful vehicle took me to the Motor Show at Olympia in the morning, then on to the Central Hall, Westminster, for the annual Missionary Meetings in the afternoon and evening; home by midnight, both car and driver well and truly flogged.

To go back; a word now about my first experience of those meetings at Westminster, when still a small boy. I had often wanted to see London and this treat my father decided to give me, having in mind to visit places of interest to us both, but including the Missionary Meetings. This gathering of close on three thousand people was something this ten-year-old found very interesting; indeed, exciting! But there was, however, a vexing incident that took away some of my pleasure. I must explain:

My sister Ruth had, to my young mind, a rather difficult personality. Though weak in body she was very strong-willed. Now I was going to be doing something she had never been able to do: I was going to London first and it was going to give me the greatest pleasure in telling her so the next time we met! Sitting in the gallery, near one of its many doors and enthralled by all I saw and heard, to my utter dismay I was suddenly confronted by this very person, who later told me that her train from Poole had arrived at Waterloo an hour before ours! To say I was disappointed to see Ruth there is to understate the effect it had upon the pride and self-satisfaction that I had been building up in my mind! I never knew if my father was party to what I perceived as a mean trick, but the next time I refer to my sister in the memoir it must be on a more favourable note!

However, I look back with pleasure to those meetings in the Central Hall, seeing and listening to people whose names were familiar through that valuable monthly, *Echoes of Service,* Bath. One after another would speak of God's blessing on their work, sometimes in the midst of much opposition. On one occasion I was very moved by hearing a man say he had not seen any conversions or baptisms since his last furlough! My verses entitled "Episcopy" (page 113) arose through that incident.

4: Formative Experiences in a Christian Home

Each time I stayed in Poole on holiday — and this could be several times a year when I was aged between ten and fourteen — it would be Grandma and Aunt Annie who would carry on the good work; so a word about those ladies will not be out of place and I find pleasure in so doing.

I never signed the pledge (a sign of abstinence in those days) but my attitude to alcohol and a decision taken in my Christian experience was in keeping with family tradition, in which drink was never a problem for it was never in the house and therefore never entered into consideration. I remember one day looking at the lovely froth on Grandma's glass of stout and pleading: "Come on, Grandma, just a sip!"

"No, no, no!" she replied, drawing it away; and this dear lady made it clear to my young mind that, had she not started taking that healthful beverage, she would not require it now! It was her medicine and her conscience was clear; but so also was her view of the suggestion sometimes made that young people should be encouraged to imbibe, but with caution! My Grandma was no fool! She was also very aware of what the Scriptures teach on Christian liberty. Paul writes: "Take heed lest by any means this liberty of yours become a stumblingblock to them that are weak" (1 Corinthians 8:9).

Grandma would have agreed with a friend who put it to me this way: he said that if in the delight of freedom I start throwing my arms about, will I please remember that my freedom ends where his nose begins!

Over the years I have felt it my duty to warn young people of seemingly harmless habits that can easily become our master. My liberty must not be allowed to hinder some poor fellow that has difficulty in getting clear of his problem. I realise increasingly that we all, in one way or another, follow others in this, and our Lord's words are relevant in speaking of the shepherd and his sheep. We bear the marks of someone we follow, for better or otherwise. On this point Mother and I were often at variance. Pleading "Mr X does it" was never to my advantage, and it mattered little if the person named was a very worthy man — I was to follow his good points!

For example, one person in particular comes to mind. Mr Will Perry had a hair style which appealed to me immensely: it was so smooth that a fly would have slid off the side; so a tin of vaseline was emptied on my hair with marvellous effect! But not for long, because my protestation, "But Mr Perry does it!" only hastened the vigorous use of a towel, even though he was a preacher of some reputation and a man of the highest integrity! I probably said to Mother that I would tell him, but, in fact, left it for seventy years before doing so. And when I did, just before he died, he told me he got the idea from the fellow above him in the office! He was a dear friend and an example to follow in ways other than hair style! Interestingly, he used to lecture on bee-keeping, though he had never himself kept bees in his life! I visited his sister recently whom I had not met until his death; it gave her joy to hear me speak of the man I knew so well and who, with others, influenced my life for good. His wife had been converted under Uncle John's ministry when she was about sixteen.

Father being away most of the time, it was Mother who carried the responsibility of sorting out the problems. She was not far from the truth when she sometimes said, "I can read you like a book!" She was a true Scott by nature, as well as by name, extremely sensitive, a rigid Sabbatarian, and a woman of her word — as I have cause to remember! In fact, I was sure it would never happen, she wouldn't dare, but I must have had my mouth open a wee bit too wide, because a well-soaped flannel was not just pushed into my mouth but did its cleaning job while there as an object lesson in the need to remedy bad language! I don't recall swearing at Mother again! She was very loyal when I exhibited a contrite spirit, and Father's heavy hand was not called for on every occasion. I repeat, she was the best mother in the world, and I like to remember that it was Mother that led me to Jesus for the forgiveness of my sins — some months before the mouthwash episode.

In speaking of Father, perhaps this verse of Scripture will be relevant: "He who spares the rod hates his son, but he who loves him is careful to discipline him". It is taken from the Book of Proverbs (chapter 13, verse 24) in which much advice is given to sons! Father clearly saw that a loving God chastens his children. This is a neglected subject to which I must return. Consistent with that he recognised the need to chasten me on occasions.

On one such occasion, mother had received a lot of abuse from her 'big boy' and it had been made very clear to me what this would entail. Father was informed on his return and was so angry that he refrained from taking action until I came home from school later in the day. Of course, another reason for the delay was to give me time to think. School must have gone hard that afternoon, but what I do remember is that, after the prescribed punishment, we both wept in each other's arms!

Some have referred to Father as being a hard man, but I insist that was not the only side of his character, as the above incident, and others to follow, make clear; and I would ask my readers to judge whether the new laws being laid on us today, though perhaps right in their objective, do not in fact tend to inhibit effective correction. Father was not a cruel man: far from it, his use of the stick was closely connected with his love for his Lord. I shall refer to his tears again.

I have mentioned Mother's extreme sensitivity, though this was probably no different from those with whom she moved and reflected the somewhat excessive prudishness of the Victorian age. I recall her being very upset when a preacher read the latter half of Romans chapter 1. Neither did she receive much comfort from Father, who agreed with the preacher. If these verses are omitted today, explanation would be asked, and not without reason.

In case the picture that has been given thus far is of a hard, unbending man (and 'tis true he drove his car like Jehu — 2 Kings 9:20!), many will support me when I say that he was a great encourager. The teachers in his Sunday School thought well of him, as indeed did he of them, for he would draw out their best. Personal work was his strong point and on that subject he would say (and I would endorse), "It may lack limelight, but not delight!"

On one occasion in my early preaching days I wanted to make clear to my listeners that being brought up in a Christian home does not make one a Christian. "In my case", I said, "it had the opposite effect!" Father, who was sitting at the rear of the chapel, must have been very much awake, for he let out a gasp so loud that all were alerted! By my unfortunate exaggeration I had given altogether the wrong impression about my home life, but this timely interjection by Father enabled me to clarify the point and add that repentance and faith in the Lord Jesus is the starting point in the Christian life.

It would be quite wrong to give the impression that upbringing had no effect, and this will be clear to my reader. Sad indeed is the position of some known to me who have turned their backs on godly training. This does not mean that I would subscribe to all that was said and practised, which at times bordered on a rather rigid narrow-mindedness, but I am sure no harm came to me as a result of misguided zeal (if that is what it was)! As an aside, Mother was way out of present-day thinking in giving me a tablespoon of castor oil when I was peevish, my real trouble being above my neck; nevertheless, it controlled my movements for a few hours!

Formative Experiences in a Christian Home

I shall be giving in some detail impressions made on me when still under eight years of age. Basic truths concerning God's holiness and my sinful nature were not omitted for fear of the poor little boy being frightened! For example, the sufferings of Jesus on the cross, His death and resurrection, and especially His coming again for those who are ready, and the punishment of the wicked, were made very clear, and on many occasions I was indeed very frightened. In no way do I hold it against my parents in this matter; they were doing the job entrusted to them and, by the mercy of God, it is to their credit that I hold as firmly as they to the 'unerringness' of the Scriptures. I have increasingly come to know the Author and Planner of history; it is the history of Redemption. These were the truths I listened to as a boy, and not all was lost, I am sure.

On every occasion possible I was taken to special meetings convened for the older generation. These were large gatherings and, whilst the needs of children were not particularly catered for, I was thrilled with the singing, new faces and surroundings; not Sunday School standard, maybe, but very nice!

In short, my spiritual life was bound up with that of my parents: I went where they went, and no thought was given to pushing me off while they fed on the things of God. I was not given all I wanted, and therefore was delighted with what I had. 'Tis true I found it hard telling the headmaster I was not playing football in the last term; if I had, I am sure he would have found some boots for the match, something Father found difficult.

Being nurtured in the fold of those who do not object to being known as Brethren, so long as it is understood to be a Christian community, a brief outline of their faith and practice will be of interest. I shall deal with only the last hundred years or so but a book by E. H. Broadbent, *The Pilgrim Church*, covering the period going back to the first century, makes profitable reading.

In the early days, the buildings where they met for worship and evangelistic outreach were known as Gospel Halls. Each church is entirely autonomous with no appointed minister; elders being responsible under the guidance of the Holy Spirit. Adult baptism, at the request of the person concerned, is practised, and the Lord's Table for remembrance is observed on Sunday.

The final authority of the Scriptures on matters of doctrine is very carefully set out in their Deeds of Trust. Generally speaking, a welcome is given to all who love the Lord as they worship, and, in this context, they are often referred to as "Open Brethren". The term "Plymouth Brethren" is misleading, savouring of restrictive practices. In evangelistic work, they have fellowship with all who are like-minded in matters of doctrine. In missionary activities, they have been outstanding world-wide. From the middle of the last century, men and women have gone to all parts with the gospel, in dependence on the Lord for their support. My heart is still with the people mentioned and, as I recall boyhood days, it will be appreciated that early impressions remain.

I invite my reader to come with me to Ebenezer Hall, Shaftesbury — the boys at school called it the "Tin Tabernacle"! — the occasion being a worship meeting just after the First World War. It will cause a smile, no doubt, but the picture I wish to draw is one of simplicity of worship as seen through the eyes of a small boy of seven or eight years old, and which perhaps harks back in some way to New Testament times when the church met in people's homes; although this is a small group meeting in a large chapel.

As we enter, a text meets the eye: "Behold the Lamb of God which taketh away the sin of the world." The colour of the words ("sin" is in black), and the number of letters, occupy my attention when there are long pauses between hymns, prayers or readings (for which no order of service is prearranged). As we sit around the table, on which are

Formative Experiences in a Christian Home

a loaf, a decanter of wine and a large metal cup, members are sitting facing each other. This enables me to watch intently their devotions (and I am glad on those occasions I was allowed to keep my eyes open — at least, I was not discouraged!).

Some of the ladies are wearing veils (I never knew why), Mother being one of them. These are pulled tight under the chin, then, prior to partaking, would be rolled up. To me these solemn activities are very interesting. Two people in particular take my attention. The little old lady facing us lives in a huge house in the centre of town — a house completely devoid of comfort. Occasionally we are invited to tea but the bread is cut too thick for the cake! Mother also has a problem because, in contrast to our cottage, this house lends itself to a marvellous echo when I shout!

Illness has affected both her voice and her features very severely, but both she and Mother are strongly attached to each other. This puzzles me, for I do not yet appreciate that they have much in common, worship being their highest exercise.

There she is, and, as she has no veil, I can see and hear her as she worships. She is radiant with joy but her singing seems to come from the deep (as indeed it did!). However, Mother's lovely contralto is rising to the occasion, so all is well.

The other person I see is old Mr Morris, a retired postman who has cycled several miles to meet with his Lord. Rising from his chair, he goes to the table. He has no gift for speaking, so his words are few, which I remember very clearly. His face is beaming as he takes and breaks the loaf, then passes it for all to partake, after which the plate is returned to the table. A few moments of quietness follow, during which I can see eyes are shut but some lips are moving. Then he rises again and pours wine from the decanter into the cup with few, but relevant, words, and all partake. I watch as each takes a sip and passes it on.

The devotion of these followers of Jesus leaves a deep impression on my young mind, and I long to know more of the real meaning of worship.

* * * * *

The reality of such worship was one of the factors which bore fruit in bringing me to the Lord. Six years later, in company with another boy in the Sunday School, one Roy Snook who was my senior by four years, I was baptised and joined that band of worshippers as they met to remember the Lord in His death. Armed with a Bible and hymn book, they came with prepared hearts; in the former we read, "Let all things be done decently and in order" (1 Corinthians 14:40), and, in the latter, Mrs Peters has given us:

> O Lord we know it matters nought
> How sweet the sound may be,
> No hearts but by the Spirit led
> Make melody to Thee.

The singing was unaccompanied, and if the wind was in the east, we would often hear music coming from a church close by. To me it sounded superb, but I found Mother did not share that view. In fact, she doubted if it went "higher than the ceiling" — very strange to me at the time, when I could hear it away down the road! I knew nothing then of how the Lord's Supper was celebrated in that church, conducted in very ornate surroundings and with a kind of pageantry far removed from that which I had witnessed where no priest in vestments was needed, and where the Lord Jesus Himself was present to lead and accept the worship of His loved ones, for whom it was a foretaste of heaven found nowhere else.

Sunday evening was the time for preaching the gospel and if there was no interesting story I was permitted to sleep. However, good preachers like Mr Meader the new postmaster would take note of small boys and this sweet little story I recall:

A company of old men had met for Evensong, but what was once a joy to hear was that no longer; so a choir of boys are invited to provide the quality of tone so sadly lacking, and again singing of a standard not heard for years fills the chapel. However, as they file out they are confronted by an angel who challenges them: "How is it there is no song for me tonight?"

Sitting still for an hour in chapel was not the only occasion for that exercise, for it was Mother's idea of a very effective punishment! It meant supervision, but I know I provided her with something that gave her a mixture of apprehension and joy in the way that hour was spent. A hymn book was essential (because I could sing as well as Mother!), also a crust of bread and a cup of water were all that were necessary for a worship meeting! Both of us were to learn years later that some of the lads in France were doing what I was doing, and with the same materials, crouched in a trench with shells flying above them — only they were doing it because they loved the Lord Jesus.

There were wonderful compensations for being still for an hour in Chapel. The Sunday School outing was an event to be remembered; a day at Wardour Castle or Melbury Hill, to which we were taken in a horse-drawn vehicle, was great fun, even though it was useless on hills! A trip by charabanc to Bournemouth was extra special; a brave man was that garage proprietor who took us there and back! I wanted to be a big, important man like that because, on the way to school, I thought he looked fine in his overalls. The grease and grime would be no hardship to me; in fact, I reasoned, people can see that you are working; and, of course, there is something else in favour of that occupation. Years later, when complaining to a farmer about the mess his vehicle deposited on the workshop floor, he replied, "Don't you know, where there's dirt, there's money?"

More recently, I received a much happier reminder

about dirt. "Oh, John, do you remember making mud pies with me in the road?" I did remember the girl, Sybil Jones, who lived the other side of our field, but not that episode! I was thrilled to meet her again and to discover that she was a believer. On hearing that her brother, Stanley Jones, was still living, though a very sick man, I made a special journey to Shaftesbury to visit him; this was a few weeks before he died. He was very pleased to see me after a lapse of nearly fifty years. He told me his school record for the 'hundred yards' was held until just a few years back. He also told me of the very full life he had had with his wife, now deceased. No family responsibilities, they had decided, were to be for them: they were going to travel. But, he added, "I tell you this, John, we both deeply regretted our selfish life-style. We had all we went in for and it left us empty!" As my family were waiting in the car my time with him had to be short, but he listened attentively as I told him of what the Lord Jesus meant to me, and left him a "Reason Why" which he said he would read. The visit was followed with a prayer that his name that for years was inscribed on the school plaque would now be written in heaven along with mine, all by the mercy of God.

Cover-up

Still thinking of my Sunday School days, we seem to hear much these days about 'cover-ups'. It would seem to be the kind of news for which people have an insatiable interest, especially if the person subjected to exposure is of note. Those who feel this dubious course of concealment by deceit is necessary will find it prudent to follow it through with care, for a lie has to be covered . . . and covered . . . and covered again. As a ten-year-old I could see that one, though I have learned a lot since then and am still learning! I was *not* a nice boy, and was quite capable of doing something to cover my guilt by ensuring the blame fell on someone else!

Formative Experiences in a Christian Home

A visiting speaker to the Sunday School told us he was going to speak about 'nothing', and that would give us fun when Mum or Dad asked about the lesson! He gave us three texts, the first two of which were spoken by the Lord to his disciples. Luke 12 verse 2 reads: "There is *nothing* covered that shall not be revealed or hid that shall not be made known." I will come back to the other two later. But when the class was over I would normally be free for the next hour or so — that is to say, as far as my best suit would allow! On this occasion, we wandered too far and so a short cut back had to be made at the double. All would have been well if the farmer had used other than barbed wire to fill the gap; as it was, the short cut ended with the same on my seat! Oh, my flesh was intact, but not my trousers; and, to make matters worse, the tear was not nice and straight but hung like a leaf. Being the guardian of my best suit, what was my story to be? Perhaps it was that the other boy pushed me; perhaps it was all the farmer's fault! In the end, confused thinking gave place to careful planning (in which Mother was not consulted), and her work basket provided all that was necessary for me to do a 'first class' repair job . . . at least, when I held it up to the light, I couldn't see through it! So, a carefully folded suit was placed in its drawer and the work basket was returned to its place.

"Glad to see you putting your clothes away, John" said Mother, some days later. My reply . . . or perhaps there wasn't one, because I had just discovered to my horror, when standing in front of a mirror and holding Mother's large hand mirror behind me, that my jacket ws too short to hide the 'repair' unless I bent over backwards; also, my braces must be pulled up much too tight for comfort. I was a very unhappy boy, and it was all the farmer's fault — except that, of course, I had been trespassing!

"Why are you walking like that? Are you in pain? Walk properly!" said Mother, when I was foolish enough to walk in front of her. A bad conscience is very painful and I was very sad until a week or so later my cover-up came to light and Mother's love and skill enabled me to walk erect without being crippled by fear. More about a 'cover-up' later, but now back to our lesson on 'nothing'. This one also came from the lips of Jesus: "A certain creditor had two debtors, and one owed five hundred pence and the other fifty, and when they had *nothing* to pay he frankly forgave them both" (Luke 7:41-42).

I am sure, in the light of my experience, I was happy to tell Mother about that story, and really therein lies the object of this memoir, to testify to our spiritual bankruptcy and to demonstrate the importance of the doctrine of the atonement.

All I remember of that Sunday School lesson are the three texts, but no doubt the speaker enlarged on the last one, as I do now. They were the words of rebuke addressed by one of the thieves to his companion crucified with him. At first, both had joined with the crowd in their insults to the Man on the centre cross, but now the heart of this man was touched by what he saw and heard. He recognised who Jesus was, and called him Lord, acknowledging his sin in these words: " . . . we receive the due reward of our deeds: but this man hath done *nothing* amiss. And he said unto Jesus, Lord, remember me when thou comest into thy kingdom" (Luke 23:41-42).

Matthew says of the soldiers that carried out this method of execution: "And sitting down they watched him there" (Matthew 27:36).

Why was he there, the sinless Son of God? I reply with the deepest conviction: He was there making a covering for my sins by taking my place and exposing Himself to the wrath of a holy God. The Scriptures are so clear on this. It is God alone who must do the covering because it is He that has been sinned against. When a man sees his true position as did this thief, and with repentance seeks God's mercy, God honours his faith and covers his sins by blotting them out by way of atonement.

Formative Experiences in a Christian Home

This is the gospel as I understand it: good news of how sinners may be reconciled to God; salvation through the death of a sinless substitute.

To many, this doctrine of the atonement is repugnant and the mention of the blood is repelling. It is invariably accompanied by rejection of the biblical doctrine of sin and redemption; no argument will touch them, only the Spirit of Truth Himself can do so.

Getting back to the years that followed boyish pranks, the Lord has found it necessary to bring home to me from time to time the words of Solomon: "He that covereth his sins shall not prosper, but he that confesseth and forsaketh his sins shall find mercy" (Proverbs 28:13).

His father, David, knew what he was talking about when he said (or sang): "Blessed is he whose transgression is forgiven and whose sin is covered" (Psalm 32:1).

David rightly placed his faith on the blood shed in sacrifice, but I often sing with deep thankfulness:

But richer blood has flowed from nobler veins
To purge the soul from guilt and cleanse the reddest stains.
(H. Bonar)

* * * * *

THE FINDING

I heard about Jesus
For widespread His fame.
But yet did not know Him,
Or value His Name.
Some knew Him to speak to,
To them He was real.
For this a deep longing
Would o'er my heart steal.

So full of frustration,
Defeated, depressed,
I needed the Saviour,
I wanted true rest.

To self held in bondage
I longed to be free.
How little I knew that
He longed to have me.

Then one day I saw Him.
I felt I must pray.
A moment of crisis,
Oh, mem'rable day!
My heart was affected
And contrite became.
He called me — I followed,
All praise to His Name!

* * * * *

Interest in music and verse

Whilst on holiday in Rye, Sussex, and sitting in a cornfield reading a magazine, I came across these words: "God deals in grace with sinners that repent", and it came to me that this was something to sing about. Before we left the field I was able to put some order to my thoughts, with the hope that a tune would come likewise whilst sitting at the piano.

From about the age of ten I had found pleasure in harmonising on piano or organ, but Father had no cash to spare in providing lessons for a lazy boy. It all started when we left Layton for Rock Cottage and where — often sitting in the dark with fingers and feet working hard — I would entertain Mother with music from an old, but very good, organ that Grandma wisely left behind for my use. I am still unable to read music, so the dozen or so hymns that have found their way to the printer have done so by the help of friends. This was necessary because they told me I used far too much sugar! My improvisations often had a sequel, and, on occasions when I seemed to have struck the very harmony of heaven, someone with an ear for good music (!) would spoil it all by saying, "That was good, play that bit again!" I leave my reader to judge what spiritual lessons I still need to learn from all this! Now for the hymn, to which I have given the title:

LOVE'S INFINITUDE

God deals in grace with sinners that repent,
    Amazing grace!
It springs from love, their blessing its intent,
    Amazing love!
How so, when justice says thy sins will find thee out?
For me, the blood of Jesus has expelled that doubt.

Yes, from that cross where God and I did meet,
    An awful cross!
And from the place where I fell at His feet,
    Oh blessed place!
I turned, not back, but only to pass on, and lo,
Alive! the One Who died because He loved me so.

Why should I doubt His power and be afraid?
    A sinful doubt.
Why should the foe attempt to ply his trade?
    A beaten foe.
Yes, why indeed! for in the power of endless life
Christ lives! and that for me shall be the end of strife.

Dear Friend, I have concern about your soul;
    A deep concern.
I'm wondering if you know Christ makes men whole?
    You ought to know.
Stretch out your hand in faith to Him Who loves you so,
And His pierced-hands-of-Love will never let you go.

* * * * *

Concerning Sundays

My early teaching on Sunday being a sabbath of rest is expressed in lines quoted by Mother on occasions; the first two lines will suffice: "Sunday is God's holy day, we must neither work nor play". I got that message right enough, but found it a bit unfair to have to sit through three meetings, when Mother had only two! I hasten to add that, whilst I was at Sunday School, she was visiting old people in the infirmary wing of the workhouse (as it was then known) and this entailed a long walk. The bicycle used six days of the week was kept in the shed until Monday. The "Boy's Own Paper", together with other interesting things, was likewise shelved.

I look back with gratitude to both parents for the way they did their best to make compensation for the lack of freedom enjoyed by other boys. No doubt my reader will be asking if we pressed these restrictions on our own children. We certainly did as a principle, bending perhaps on points, and up to the time of writing no word of reproach has reached my ear! Gentle persuasion needed to be used at times! I would remind them of the message God sent to Eli: " . . . them that honour Me I will honour" (1 Samuel 2:10).

The point made was that our treasures put aside on the Lord's Day increase in value. I shall return to this later in my story because it had an important effect on my business life (for being closed on Sunday actually brought in business); meanwhile, a word about that quotation. The story of Eli is a sad one: here is a godly man, and a priest of Israel, who loved the Lord but failed miserably in the exercise of proper authority over his two sons whom he loved. They, in turn, became callous and lost all respect for their father. The end of their life (and his) was tragic.

Concerning motors

Being a motor racing fan, my school days had their thrills because, living near Spread Eagle Hill, we would on occasions see Malcolm Campbell, Raymond Mayes, Frazer Nash, and others of that calibre, vie for the fastest time. I was able to see that the spectacular gave lots of excitement but was no winner. It was the man who could keep his wheels on the ground that got the points.

Later, after five years in the workshop engaged mainly on repairs to vehicles used for business, I found myself completely weaned from any interest in that particular sport. Life was more serious now, with long hours of work and other responsibilities. Cars had other uses.

Collecting a car for service, one of my staff came back with this one: The owner, together with her mother who is holding the cat, are standing in the drive watching his departure. But not until advice was given in terms to be remembered: "You be careful with me car, young man, it's me life!" Then, quickly correcting herself, she added, "I mean, me life is me mother, me cat and me car!"

Much that follows covers the years when motor sales and service occupied most hours of the day and when I was "on my own". There are few jobs which have so much potential for things to go wrong, and many a time I wished I had never started and had to remind myself of Who it was that put me there. But this is going ahead, and I must go back.

5: Into the Fray

I now come to an event that took place while I was still at school and in my early 'teens, and one that was to remind me that I was not my own, I belonged to Christ. Believing it to be an act clearly taught in the New Testament that called for obedience on my part, I submitted to baptism by immersion, along with Roy Snook, an older boy mentioned already and who will appear later in my story. It was a witness to the world that we were followers of the Lord Jesus.

We were then received into fellowship with the Lord's people and took our place at His Table. Of the real significance of baptism I had much to learn, and will return to the subject again; but for me, the battle was now on!

Academically, I was slow and needed pushing, and this Father did with some effect! I was to choose a career from which there would be no turning back! There were good reasons for his insistence on my sticking to the job because several of his contemporaries were able to finance every whim their sons came up with! He thought this was for my good, as indeed it was, and I am grateful for it. But no doubt his position demanded it. I am sure both he and Mother breathed a sigh of relief when my interest in going to sea switched to motor cars and bikes.

An old friend of the family had bought a new Chevrolet open tourer from a garage in Parkstone, and made an enquiry on my behalf; the result being that the Motor Trade was to be my lot and Parkstone the place where, for the next three years, I would learn the trade ... and also discover the depravity of my heart!

I thought I was well-prepared: I was going to 'nail my colours to the mast', which I did and, right away, began to witness for the Lord — quite unaware the devil was hot on my track! He is not almighty, but his power must never be belittled.

My place of work was situated behind a public house. My pay was five shillings for the forty-eight hour week, plus twopence an hour overtime. For several months I stayed with my Grandma and Aunt in Poole and later moved into lodgings; but, as my parents had moved from Shaftesbury to Swanage, I was able to go home at weekends.

The next part of my story I would like to skip, but it will be seen to have an important bearing on the following years in my contact with young people.

I thought the bad language and dirty talk heard at school was the limit; but now, with girls slipping in from the bar to talk to the fellows, a new dimension of wickedness presented itself. At first I was very shocked; but that soon wore off and it was not long before I was all ears and my pathway became very dangerous; in fact, I was giving more thought to their conversations than to my job!

My dear ones at home had no idea that I was in such deep water but I know now that I had their prayers, and this will be seen in what follows.

For me as a Christian they were bad days indeed, but they also formed a necessary turning point in my spiritual experience, the first move coming from an unexpected quarter — as so often happens when God is at work. The truth is, the young man that came home each weekend was not the same man in the workshop during the week. I knew it, the staff knew it, and my boss knew it — and it was he who, on one 'ever-to-be-remembered' occasion, drew my attention to it. It happened in this way:

I had found myself at odds with the storekeeper, a little fellow about half my size, and who, no doubt, was not privileged to start the day on bacon and egg; but he was good at his job, perhaps too good for me! (My friends in the motor trade will agree that the counter between stores and workshop needs to be a wide one!) Just outside the Governor's office is a foolish place for a punch-up, but, with temper running high, I stepped towards him, shouting, "I'm going to punch your **** nose!" My well-chosen adjective, however, lost all its significance because my action was suddenly halted when the boss appeared in the doorway and, looking at me with a sickly smile, said, "Was that the text on Sunday, Jack?" He was in the habit of expressing himself in similar terms, as indeed was Felix, the storekeeper, who was now grinning at my discomfiture, the little wretch still being in one piece! Before I finish the story, we will see him again in a different setting.

But it was not only the Governor's voice that I heard that day (plus that of Satan, rubbing it in!): the tender voice of my Lord was telling me I could not do it alone — I needed Him. It was certainly a day of reckoning, and one in which I asked Him to take over; and He has been true to His word, saving me from calamity.

To his credit, Father had done his best to warn me; in fact he had been very explicit in speaking of the power wielded by drink and sex. But here I was, still 'covering up' at home, while in fact I was in a state of mental turmoil through being in the thick of the temptations presented by both! Furthermore, each weekend I was taking a Sunday School class. Had I felt able to share my problem with him, Father would have been to me a tower of strength; instead, it was people outside the family circle who sensed I needed help and laid themselves out to give it. This was the way God was going to answer my prayer. Some might call what happened to me a second conversion, and, if they are right, I have had a number! On this I am clear: the arm of the Lord and the chastening hand of my heavenly Father, together with the prodding of His Holy Spirit upon my conscience, are the prime factors in my finding victory through these temptations. To be told by a man sixty years later that he still remembers things I said which helped him in that Sunday class, is beyond me!

Into the Fray

I still need to keep myself in the love of God, as Jude put it: "looking for the mercy of our Lord Jesus Christ" (Jude 21). Paradoxical it may seem, but left to myself I am unable to keep myself. So a question arises that actually indicates the answer: "Do I love Jesus enough to want Him to do it for me?" Someone has coined the phrase "the expulsive power of the new affection" to describe the victory which can be gained over sin through loving submission to Jesus, who is longing and looking for contrite hearts that open to him.

Now a word about my 'come-back' as the sun now breaks through and beams on my dial! First a word about my job which will serve to introduce the point I wish to make. At that time, all Chevrolets were fitted with a huge undertray that was intended to catch oil, or anything else, from the engine. In practice, however, it also collected matter deposited on the road by four-legged creatures! It was my job to remove this ridiculous item, to enable the mechanic to gain access to the engine, and then clean it before replacing — "clean enough to eat your dinner off it!" As it would meet the customer's eye when he lifted up the bonnet, my boss made sure his eye was on it before the car left the garage.

On one occasion I not only got it hot from the boss, but the same again from my landlady: "bad odour" was not the phrase she used!

I have referred to people who have gone out of their way to help me, no doubt constrained by love to Christ, and I am thinking of one couple in particular, Mr and Mrs George Price by name, who invited me to spend the Sunday with them in Pokesdown. It was a happy time in which I, with a certain self-importance over the vast knowledge acquired through two years in the motor trade, was able to speak about my work to good listeners, though no doubt omitting the bit about undertray cleaning! These kind friends were taking it all in for what it was worth, at the same time seeking guidance for the right word with which to send me on my way. It is this that stands out in my memory. For as I was about to board the tram for Parkstone my friend hung on to my hand for his parting shot: "Goodbye, Jack, keep busy, it will keep you clean." Bumping about on the top of that tram, the rhythm of the wheels on the track joints fitted the words perfectly along with those of Mother, "Satan finds mischief for idle hands to do"! That Sunday evening I felt more ready for the battle ahead, and I would urge young Christians to get involved in work for the Lord. It must be a wholehearted commitment and requires definite action.

A large notice in a joiner's workshop once caught my attention, "Do your cleaning up while you work." And it was along this line that my boss told me to "clean the corners and the rest will clean itself".

With over sixty years behind me I still have reason to sing (at times with some emotion):

>   *Search all my thoughts, the secret springs*
>   *The motives that control;*
>   *The rebel heart where evil things*
>   *Hold empire o'er the soul.*
>
>   *Search, till Thy fiery glance has cast*
>   *Its holy light through all,*
>   *And I by grace am brought at last*
>   *Before Thy face to fall.*
>
>   *Thus prostrate I shall learn of Thee*
>   *What now I feebly prove,*
>   *That God alone in Christ can be*
>   *Unutterable love.*
>
>   (F. Bottome)

Often, working long hours, there was little free time, but I was given wisdom to meet with Christians of my own age and who were facing the same enemy; and we were often privileged to listen to faithful preachers, gifted to touch where it hurt while at the same time presenting

Into the Fray

Christ in such a way that one was drawn and not repelled.

I have recently renewed contact with one such brother in Christ, and what joy it gave us! Frank Lawes, five years my senior, well remembers speaking in the little wooden hut erected in Corfe Castle about the year 1926, but does not recall my presence or indeed his message. My memory serves me well for once, because I not only didn't like the content, but I objected to his eye resting on me while he delivered it! Of course, I had to agree that his eye had to rest somewhere! The fact was, his ministry touched my conscience. The hour together was very precious and we parted with hearts full of thankfulness to our Father for His tender dealings with us both.

Yearly meetings held in the Bournemouth area for Sunday School teachers were outstanding in providing help and encouragement for workers among young people. Much of the ministry was very searching and hard-hitting. I recall one speaker giving a vivid picture of a lazy teacher who was too tired to do his homework! I am sure his eye never left me until I had got the message! However, I found some relief and comfort at the break for tea in hearing that others had also taken a knock!

Special weekends were arranged when it was kept in mind that man is a tripartite being, made up of body, soul and spirit, each of which God has provided for. Some outstanding occasions come to mind when I listened to the word of God opened up by those who had a real experience of life, as well as of the Scriptures; also, I might add, many of these were young people not much my senior! Places like Grittleton, Brockenhurst, Oxford, quickly come to mind.

Possibly someone reading this would tell us that it was at one of these conventions that he met the one who was to join him in a life partnership, and for which the subject matter was very relevant. Outside the assembly room things could be hilarious, and also during a session some brightness would creep in; but when the message was being put across there would be no mistake as to whether the speaker was serious or not! The organised fun and games were great, but it was usually with subdued spirits that we came out from those talks.

It has been my experience that much of the teaching received in early days lies dormant until required, and then it appears with a freshness upon our spirit. I thank God for those men and women who laid it on for us: leaders they were, indeed.

Many young people are at a cross-roads in their careers and not all have wise parents to guide them. Those were good opportunities to be taken aside for a quiet chat, leaders sometimes passing one on to another better versed in a particular problem. A lot of follow-up work, too, was put into it.

Some of my contemporaries were seriously considering serving the Lord overseas and there were occasions when workers from abroad were able to speak of how the Lord was leading them.

One young fellow from overseas was speaking about problems in presenting the gospel to the people in his area. His English was very good but his choice of words was (for him) unfortunate, as it affected several of his listeners. If he had said "uneducated peasants" it would have passed without a murmur, but "ignorant farmers" brought the roof down in a storm of (good humoured) protest! For a while he couldn't continue, but when someone explained to him his 'faux pas' he took it in good part.

With others about this time, I was passing through that adolescent stage when personal appearance was given undue attention. Of course they do today, but it seems there is a difference in taste — a neighbour told me recently that her son was angry because she dared to repair a tear in his shirt! But in my day it was the 'Fifty Shilling Tailor' that made an appeal. This 'oil rag' that left the garage at midday on Saturday would be seen in the afternoon dressed in black jacket and pin-stripe trousers, butterfly collar with bow tie, and bowler hat (which, sad to say, showed the rain-spots, unlike my friend's velour, whose wage packet was fatter!).

I was aware that dowdiness does not commend itself, but I needed to remember that, for the Christian, neither does ostentation: both draw attention unduly to oneself. An evangelist friend of mine passed this on for my benefit, for whom a timely rebuke from his wife went like this:

"Hurry up, Darling, we shall be late. What are you doing?"

"Getting myself ready; you want people to see me looking nice, don't you?"

"If it's only that which you want people to see, that's all they will see!"

For some months I stayed in the same digs as Roy Snook, the friend referred to previously. Roy, four years my senior, helped me a lot in my hour of need. He understood my difficulties, having had problems of his own while working as a grocer; but while I was in the doldrums spiritually he, by contrast, was making progress and was able to take a lead in our reading and praying together. The landlady and her husband attended the same church as ourselves. Our stay with them terminated because some water

This 'Oil Rag'!

that was being carried upstairs spilled over on to the head of our landlady as she stood at the bottom! Who it was that held the glass, or jerked the other's arm, was never gone into!

Some years later I found myself sitting in a large meeting, feeling quite safe, until the lady sitting in front of me turned and said, "It's John, I believe!" In my confusion I blurted out, "Have you forgiven me?" Her smile and reply put me right and, after the service, it was a joy to share news of our families.

We never met again, but many years later I received a message from her husband, now living alone, saying he wanted to see me. I think I should just say here that I always felt he had made some contribution to our exuberance! We were delighted to see each other once more, and this time not under a cloud. He told me that, after we had left, they joined another church of what I speak of sometimes as the "Enthusiastics" and had spoken in tongues on many occasions. My knowledge of this being second-hand only, I asked him to enlarge, and was very surprised to hear him say, emphatically, that his experience had not been of the Lord. As I pressed him further, he said that self-control was never present and, this being one of the fruits of the Spirit, he could now see that he had missed his way. This brings to mind hearing a young woman giving her testimony and saying that, when this gift that she had been praying for came upon her, she could not stop giggling! I saw my friend on two further occasions, and each time was, for me, a benediction and contained an important lesson. The devil may be able to counterfeit the gifts of the Spirit but not His fruits — they are unmistakable.

A rough ride

Before I left my first employer, I had made some progress in the workshop and my weekly wage was now twelve shillings and six pence. At that time, General Motors were assembling Chevrolets at Hendon and, as there were no transporters in those days, I must be taught to drive. Three lessons on a Chev van were all that was needed for this sixteen-year-old — and I really must blow my own trumpet here because Chevrolets were fitted with a leather cone clutch. Unless this was treated with neat's-foot oil, a kangaroo take-off was unavoidable. All was well for me because my instructor was the foreman, and, if I could start off without hitting the wall in front, I could drive!

My first driving job was to take an old Rover to Ringwood when the bridges at Longham and Ringwood were not what they are today, neither did the cars drive themselves as they do today. To speak of the good old days in motor terms is nonsense, in my view. I thought I was doing very well and so did my hard-boiled governor, who realised he was on to a good thing! And so my next thrill was to accompany an older man in collecting a Chev chassis from Hendon, all with a view to the boss getting his value for my wage! A few days later I was handed a pound note, together with a release note, and told I could keep the change! The following morning found me on the 7.30 train to Waterloo, then Underground to Hendon.

It was not long before I was doing this job several times a week, and somehow it was always a chassis that would fall to me; when the weather was cold the conditions were so bitingly harsh that I often wondered if I could stay on the seat long enough to reach the next café. It was impossible to drive fast because they had no weight to keep them on the road; you just set the hand throttle at the speed you hoped to maintain.

The novelty of this trip had worn off, and I was no longer happy in my work, feeling that advantage was being taken of me. Nor was the boss happy when I gave in my notice; indeed, he was very annoyed, having no doubt got the message of my discontent. He told me he took a dim view of my leaving after having knocked some shape into me from a poor start! He had a point, as I was to discover some years later when some of my own employees left just as they were getting useful as a result of the money and effort I had put into training them. Not long before I retired he paid a visit to our showroom, a very old man but with the same characteristic wink of the eye. I was glad to see him and to remind him of that five shillings a week, to which he replied, "Doesn't look as if it did you much harm, Jack!" Before we parted I was able to speak of the goodness of God over the years, to which he listened attentively. Maybe God had His hand on that visit after 'many days'.

From Parkstone I went to Wimborne, and for the next year I was working under a Christian master, Reg Rodway, and often went with him to weekend meetings; on one weekend he took me to his home in South Wales. His financial problems, leading to staff adjustment, brought about my move to Lee Motors in the Winton area of Bournemouth, where I once again found lodgings with my old school friend, Roy Snook.

The Triumph Seven Fabric Saloon.

6: A New Enterprise

After a year or so at Lee Motors I finally came to Swanage, where I was to follow my trade for the next three years, living under the parental roof, and working once again under a master who was a committed Christian. Mr Boxall was in his sixties and, never having learned the Motor Trade, his knowledge of internal combustion engines was nil! However, if given a square of sheet metal, hammer and anvil, he would give us in minutes a dustbin lid that would fit and would not blow off in the wind. Of course, we didn't need a dustbin lid very often and, I am ashamed to say, we often took mean advantage of his ignorance of motors! This I confessed to his daughter some years after his death. She was rather a sweet girl and had given us the impression that she was on our side; but I am sure she was loyal to her father. Before I leave him, I must point out that we had much in common; although he met with Exclusive Brethren, we were always conscious that we shared the common life in Jesus. There was one occasion when this employer had cause sharply to remind me of what is expected of a Christian when my irritation, impatience and annoyance resulted in ill-advised speech; later I was to receive the same reproof from my head mechanic, Tony. I hasten to add that this man stayed with me until retirement and, later, was regularly in my congregation, with an expression that told me he was with me!

Working in Swanage, under conditions somewhat different from those experienced previously, I embarked on a new enterprise in which 'trying it out' was never contemplated; at the age of twenty-two I began what was to be over fifty years of very happy family life. Our train passed through many a tunnel but there was always a light to be seen at the far end when we looked for it!

Through a CSSM Beach Mission a few years previously Joan Cleall had surrendered to the claims of the Lord

The author and his wife on their wedding day.

A New Enterprise

Jesus. I was at school with her brother Rosser, who was a boarder and in the same class. Like myself, he was working in Bournemouth and was being brought home each weekend by his sister, who was driving a little Triumph Seven fabric saloon — a very interesting little vehicle. I was quite taken up with both car and driver and later got to know them quite well!

Before we married, a call was made for Christian men to ply their trade overseas — in South America in particular; this was to help missionaries. We gave serious thought to going, even starting to learn Spanish with this in view. The apostle Paul plied his trade on occasions and gave sound reasons for doing so. However, the starting of a family meant our shelving this idea for the time being.

Monica, our first child, was born prior to my starting business on my own account. A year later David arrived but after a few weeks developed eczema, a complaint no doubt connected with the asthma problem that had plagued his mother during teenage. During hospital treatment that at first appeared very satisfactory he suddenly developed septicaemia, which brought about his death on Easter Day 1935. The shock of this tragedy left Joan very upset for about a year, and she was also troubled with migraines. The trauma of losing David was compounded by mounting business pressures I was beginning to encounter. I was now going to face problems very different in character from those of Parkstone days, but with the same loving heavenly Father working out my spiritual education.

Later, there were three more girls added to the family circle.

Since those days of considering serving the Lord overseas, I have had to face the question of what I understand the "Lord's work" to be. It is, for the Christian, I believe, just what he is already doing if he has sought the Lord's will for his life; and this leads me to break off my own story and return to that of my father and uncle.

I feel that what follows must be told, though it will be with a mixture of joy and sorrow, if the object of this memoir is to be fulfilled.

The author and his wife, Joan, with their four daughters (in order of age) Monica, Winifred, Mildred, Jocelyn.

A New Enterprise

A sad fall

Working as a team, it was my uncle who did most of the preaching. Father's gift was personal work, and no conversational Bible study would be dull if he could avoid it! On one such occasion, a soldier had remarked that, after his conversion, he made up his mind to carry out all that his New Testament made clear. Knowing this man to be a Salvationist, Father couldn't resist asking what action he took when he came to the subject of baptism! The poor fellow was afflicted with a bad stammer, so Father had to wait awhile for the answer, which, when it came, was brief: "I was baptised!" Father lost that one! But my guess is that, not being bogged down on the 'first principles of the oracles of God', that Bible study was well spent.

Many a letter home he wrote for men in the Royal Naval Division, most of whom never came back from the Dardanelles. Only in eternity will the results of these contacts come to light. In front of me lies an old copy of "The Traveller's Guide from Death to Life", which brings to mind that, when a boy of eight, I spent my holiday with Father on Blandford Camp and was astonished to hear that some grown-up men couldn't read! Father would use the pictures and tell the stories from that valuable little book, of which two million copies in five languages were printed. An interesting remark Mother made, some time after I left school and they were living in Swanage, was, "I didn't know your father was so gifted in opening up the Scriptures!" With a family to rear, she missed Bible teaching; nevertheless, she did a lot of 'digging' for herself.

This brings me to a very sad part of my story, the inclusion of which has required careful thought. I go back to the time when I was baptised and still at school. I had been told that my Uncle was no longer preaching, and I knew he was a sick man and often could be seen pacing up and down the hall in silence, taking no notice of me. But the real cause, a moral collapse, I was to discover only some years later. In Uncle's divinely appointed gift for working among boys and girls, the devil found a door left open through lack of prayer and watchfulness, in which he was able to put an end to a dedicated life of service for the Lord. Many of these children and their parents had come to know and love the Lord through his preaching; but now we see a broken man, taking his place in discipline, truly penitent. His fellow believers stood with him in his hour of need, as did his brother, of whom I shall have more to say.

I would like to leave this sad story just here, but find myself unable to because I feel the issues are important. It was when the church felt happy to welcome him back into full fellowship that he realised that the door for the

A New Enterprise

resumption of the same kind of full-time service was not open as before; this made him bitter and all joy was gone. His cutting himself off from those who loved him dearly caused much sorrow to many outside the family. To us, however, he remained very close. What follows in the memoir will help my reader to see why Father often spoke to me about his brother. He was right, in my judgment, in saying that, had Uncle bowed to God's leading for him, he could have given many more years of service, even if not again in the way that he had envisaged. This reminds me of a song Mother used to sing, one line of which ran, "But the bird with a broken pinion never soared so high again".

Uncle's remaining years were spent in renovating old property in the Purbeck area. Just before he died he asked me to forgive him! I was very moved by this, the truth being that I was deeply indebted to him, for without his help I would never have been able to start business on my own. For, because he was no longer preaching, he had been both available and willing to help me in those early days of the business. The Lord alone knows the many who were led to Him through Uncle's preaching; I must now tell of one.

In the early part of the war, I was preaching in the little hut erected at that time in East Morden, not far from the cottage where I was born. (The same hut eventually was brought to Harman's Cross, and appears again in the narrative.) After the service a man asked me if I were related to the Foley brothers. He then told me of a sad home life that changed dramatically when his drunken father was converted, which took place in a meeting when the tent was at Charlton Marshall. When he told me his name I realised I knew his father well and had been to his farm as a boy on several occasions. The man I knew was a keen Christian with a large family, most of whom followed the Lord. I later had the joy of taking part in the service when this man was baptised.

Uncle's fall was a great shock to Father but he soon found that God had plans that were in character not far removed from pre-World War I days. Working in the Purbeck area of Dorset, his energies were now to be devoted to building up a church and instructing young men in preparation for full-time evangelistic work. From what has gone before it will be clear that he had much to pass on, as a number have gratefully acknowledged — the writer included.

Before marriage, I often listened to profitable talks at the meal table, and one such comes to mind. A young man from an Anglican background had spent the morning (or part of it) in visiting a young widow. No doubt he had James 1:27 in mind, but he needed to be reminded that the same chapter speaks of people needing wisdom, and this young man had already called on this needy one the previous day! This being so, Father felt it his place to pass on a word of caution. I had heard it before, and knew that Father had a point, and on that occasion it had been accepted as sound advice. But our friend thought the implication outrageous and the heat generated to flash point! Lessons go hard sometimes, and none of us enjoyed that lunch.

The subject has never left me; we are all vulnerable, and that visit should have been handled by a sister in the church; no doubt it was Mother that was in Father's mind. It was not without reason that he had strong views on what work rightly belonged to women in the church of God. More than one of his brethren had been shipwrecked whilst engaged in the Lord's work. God's Word is full of warnings and it is all too easy to become careless about our vulnerable nature.

This very accomplished young man did not stay long with us, as Mother predicted! But years later, and long after both of my parents were at Home with the Lord, a Church of England minister called on me; he had recently retired and was on his way to visit a man whom he had

A New Enterprise

led to Christ when with us — someone I knew well. He spoke in cordial terms of my parents, as our minds went back over the years, but neither of us made reference to his innocent intrusion on Mother's preserve!

This leads me to express my own thoughts on the position of women in their church life. Over the past fifty years my view has changed little on the woman's God-given role in the fellowship of His people as they worship and witness.

Their emancipation in the past two thousand years is due to the influence of the Gospel of Jesus Christ. After Pentecost, believing women took their place side by side with believing men, but it was not long before Satan was at work, as he had been in the Garden, leading Eve to act independently of Adam. New Testament writers were clear on what took place in Eden, and with good reason; it was basic to problems that had arisen; and before I leave this 'divisive' subject, I would share my experience.

For a number of years it has been my privilege to meet Saturday mornings for prayer. It is the only occasion when the sisters pray audibly (if they so wish) and it has rejoiced my heart. After a brother reads some verses of Scripture, and asks for any special matters for prayer, we not only gain information, but also a clearer understanding, of the burdens carried by some, both in the church and elsewhere. There are no long prayers, and much ground is covered on this particular occasion. For convenience, we meet in the same building (albeit a classroom) where we meet for worship, on which occasion the sisters do not pray audibly. Singing is another matter, and one which I have never heard questioned. The sisters are amazingly patient with their brothers as they wait to be led in worship, and the value of their support is great.

In the early days of the Gospel Hall in Swanage an elderly lady, who had come to live near the Mission, asked to be allowed to remember the Lord at His Table. We did not see her very often, she being in poor health, but if when she came and there was rather a long pause, she would rise to her feet and pour out her heart in worship! Being stone deaf, and the seating facing the front, she would miss much of the service if unable to see the speaker.

Father's strong views on the subject proved to be not so strong when it came to dealing with this 'departure'. As a result, he took a sharp reprimand from a visiting brother who, in turn, received this reply: "This dear saint can hear no voice except her own and the Lord has not laid it upon my heart to discourage her."

Before Father was called Home, he told me he had come to the view that the restricting of sisters, in praying and praising audibly in presence of brothers, went beyond the clear guidelines of Scripture. He would never make an issue of the matter, neither would I, and nor would the sisters referred to; harmony is too precious. Nevertheless, I think it sad that many godly sisters have never heard their own voices in prayer because they have been discouraged from doing so.

I write at a time when the ecclesiastical temperature is running high concerning the admission of women to the priesthood. For me, this presents no problem because my Bible is clear; I have no priest but Jesus my Lord, and I find it well defined when I seek to follow in obedience to His will.

Back now to my early married days and starting on my own in business.

On my own, but . . .

I have already indicated that the starting of family life was leading us to see God's hand guiding us away from serving Him abroad to witnessing for Him in the business world. Accommodation had been provided in the form of a wood/asbestos building, once used by my wife's brother for breeding Angora rabbits! This was erected on

A New Enterprise

a plot of land owned by my uncle at Harman's Cross and made into a very comfortable dwelling. The new main road from Corfe Castle to Swanage now completed, Harman's Cross was just beginning to appear on the map. Notice was given to my employer and, with cash received from my uncle, four second-hand Bowser hand-operated pumps with tanks were purchased.

Clearing the thickly-wooded site, and excavating by hand, was a job to which my early training in the workshop had left me unsuited; I suffered an attack of lumbago, and have needed to wear a belt ever since! Still not out of the wood, when the pumps were ready for Weights and Measures testing, cash for the petrol had dried up! To make my dismay complete, a friend (!) told me he thought my project would be a flop — "Too far from the town", he said. Now my backache was followed by the jitters! However, Shell Mex didn't share his view. They filled my tanks to start me off and have been doing so for the past fifty years.

Worry, that wretched thing that our Lord spoke of as being alien to faith, I was to experience often in the days ahead; sometimes in the night, when the overdraft was at

67

its limit, with a load of petrol due in the morning. When I started to employ labour, I soon learned that other lives were bound up with mine. I was used to hand-to-mouth living — it was always God's hand and my mouth! But I could never bring myself to use that ploy with my employees to relieve myself of responsibility toward them! I look back with gratitude to the latter part of school days when feeding was frugal — it was a good start to life.

The happiest part of day-to-day business life was the occasion when it was clear that this was where God had put me to witness for Him. Helping someone out of a jam is very rewarding.

When the repair shop and petrol pumps were in service, a big notice was placed on the forecourt: "CLOSED ON SUNDAY" — and this had the effect of pulling in business during the week, when it was welcome! However, on a number of occasions, on returning from the morning service I would find a car sitting in front of my sign with its front wing resting on the wheel. One look was enough to tell me that the torsion bar was broken. Mum and Dad with a load of kids looking sad was also enough to keep my sabbatarian views in right perspective. So the question now is not, "What would Mother say?" but "What would Jesus do?" "My Sunday class is at 2 pm and I'm in my best clothes and these folks are a long way from home." The gratitude shown was no small compensation and usually gave me an opportunity to send them off with a copy of Robert Laidlaw's "The Reason Why" to read on the beach.

To put the record straight, there have been some occasions when my response to someone's needs has fallen short, and not only was I the loser, so was the Lord!

Help and encouragement

I must mention another young man who was helping Father in the Mission at Herston, Sydney Pearcey by

A New Enterprise

name, because he not only helped me in the erecting of the workshop, but later was to marry my wife's sister, Ruth. Father found him a very able preacher, while to me he was also a good electrician, plumber, bricklayer, carpenter — the lot! After the war, when we started doing body and chassis repairs, he came back as an acetylene welder. I also remember him with deep appreciation for help given at Woodside Chapel. He had his problems, and his wish to become a full-time evangelist eluded him; but I, for one, was enriched spiritually through knowing Sydney.

Father's contribution to my progress, both in business and in my spiritual life, was enormous, and I want to say plainly that the man who encouraged me to start in, and stick to, the Motor Trade was now standing by me in my effort, whilst earning a living, to serve God — something I yearned to do. For years he had attended the Home Workers Conference, held in those days in Llanfairfechan, North Wales. Who it was that pulled the strings I never asked, but when he declined the invitation it was passed on to me!

On three successive years before the war, he took my place in the garage by arriving in time to open up, as this was the only way I could be free. At that time I employed a man and a boy. Father did all the taxi work, serving petrol, and taking all the knocks!

With a mind at rest, I found myself sitting at the feet of a very gifted teacher of God's Word, whose main theme was "The Gospel and its Message". It was a time when I was to learn much that was to be with me for life, and I am unable to resist naming three who helped me greatly — W. E. Vine, H. StJohn and Dr A. Rendle Short. I will be ever grateful to the latter for pressing us to obtain "In Understanding Be Men" by T. C. Hammond. Each time I returned from Plas Menai, I was very aware that my knowledge of the Bible would only give power to my preaching whilst its Author is both centre and circumference to its presentation.

Before leaving speaking about my father and my indebtedness to him, I recall that many years later, and long after business had grown and Father was Home with his Lord, a caller enquired after "the little old man with the white nanny beard"! She said she remembered his remarks when he served her. My guess is that they would have been said with that intention and would, as she pulled away, be followed by a prayer that it be so.

In the mercy of God, my upbringing provided me with a healthy fear of allowing the business side of my life to squeeze out the spiritual. I have seen this take place with others and it makes a sorry story.

For example, a man with whom for many years I had much fellowship, both in business and in the things of the Lord (more later on this), called to have a chat. He was doing very well in coach hire, but obviously at cost to his soul. His last words as he drove away were, "Pray for me, Jack". My immediate prayer was, however, "Keep your hand on *me*, Lord." The warnings of Scripture are very plain: "No man can serve two masters ... you cannot serve God and money" (Matthew 6:24).

Before my friend backslid, God used him in blessing to others; some are known to me, but I want to speak about his own conversion. Whilst he was representing a firm of Motor Factors, I asked him to call on my brother-in-law, who was then running a general store in Corfe Mullen and who wanted to widen his sales activities. His first visit — about which I never knew if he received an order! — resulted in his being invited into Sydney Pearcey's lounge where, then and there, both on their knees, he found mercy and was soundly saved. Before that, I do not recall ever speaking to him about the Lord! The ways of our God are past finding out! He preached on one occasion at Herston and, some time later, another man from the same firm, whom he had led to the Lord, also spoke at Woodside Chapel.

7: Tools of the Trade

To a reader who is conversant with motor repairs and overhauls, it will be of interest to hear about what we were doing fifty years back. Starting a business from scratch, with no services available apart from a telephone, will give some idea of the conditions we faced in those early days. Power and light were provided by a Lister engine with a fifty volt generator and batteries dating from World War I. If the rainfall was low, water was brought from Corfe Castle in a trailer with tank. These conditions were new to me and I marvel that I ever found fellows that were willing to work under them, but they did, and I will enlarge on our activities.

For some months before I left my job to start on my own, I was making a note of the tools I thought essential. It was not long, however, before I found that changes in vehicle design made many of these obsolete, and some were never used. Another thing I had to learn was that, after the initial burst of support, business does not just fall into one's lap! In fact, we had to fight for much of our business; or that is what we did! Liaison with other garages was not what it is today and I often had cause to remember some sound advice given by the last foreman I worked with: "Never run down your competitor: one day you may need his help."

Although forewarned, I had to learn this lesson the hard way and at times took on work that was beyond our ability! Before we acquired a boring bar, we were doing cylinder reboring with a hone, powered by a five-eighth inch electric drill; and a back-aching job it was, especially if done in situ. But it gave the engine a new lease of life and the customer a bill that was within his reach.

Most of the work done during the war was confined to tractors and commercial vehicles, but we later found this did not agree too well with private car work, and so it was brought to an end. We were also undertaking body work and complete re-sprays, but in premises that were totally unsuitable because of the fumes. So that work had to be put out. Again, complete engine re-conditioning was giving place to fitting replacement blocks. In short, the whole pattern of trading was changing to 'Car and Van Sales and Service', mainly under Vauxhall franchise, and with it a change in business problems. One area in which things became much easier was that of bad debt, or extended credit, as some call it! In this I have to acknowledge there were times when I was a problem to my suppliers, but on no occasion did I ever find them unreasonable. I was never told to take my business elsewhere!

On the other side of the coin, it was not often I took action against my debtors, but when I did I felt very unhappy about it. This is a delicate subject, and one in which the Lord has had to deal with me, because it is all too easy to have a blind spot, withholding payment from a forbearing creditor when it is due, in order to pay cash elsewhere, sometimes for something not actually needed; which amounts to giving generously at someone else's expense. Many non-Christians put us to shame on this matter.

In personal problems relating to the personnel side of business, a big test that our witness as Christians undergoes is how we react under pressure; can we keep our cool? Irritation can be avoided if attention is given to listening, and when time is given for this two-way understanding, a much closer relationship follows. We may be led to think that to niggle about nothing is the norm for the Motor Trade, but the truth is, customer or staff problems are real to the persons concerned. I have known the office door to open with, "Look here, Guv!", then shut with a bang when the angry man is told to come back when cooled. Half an hour later, the prepared piece begins, "Sorry about that, Guv!", and a profitable talk follows, one that good management would not ignore. We

Tools of the Trade

must be in it together, and the governor must be approachable. Closely associated with this is our ability to keep confidences, and before we start rocking the boat it will be wise to ask ourselves: "Is it true, is it kind; is it necessary?"

During the last days of the war I was collecting parts from Bournemouth and, to my surprise and joy, the man who served me was no other than the storekeeper whose nose I had threatened to punch some ten years previously! As we gripped hands I gasped, "Felix!" "No," he replied, "my name is Frank. I'm not the same man you used to know. I'm now a Christian!" I hope I didn't waste too much of his boss's time, but it was long enough to fix a date for him to preach at Swanage. I was aware of Paul's warning, "Lay hands on no man suddenly", but this was a special case and had I missed out on the last occasion! Knowing something of his background, it was a thrill to hear his clear testimony of God's saving grace.

A few months later I was best man at his wedding and well remember his instructions. I was to be ready to say my piece very clearly at the reception, because he and his bride would be the only Christians present, apart from the Vicar! It was 'sowing beside all waters' and I was glad to do this for my friend, although perhaps my "punch" was not so hard as he envisaged! This brings me back to the subject of witnessing for Christ.

I have never doubted the peril man is in if he persists in ignoring his Maker, and I fail in my duty to my fellows when I let slip the opportunities God gives me. Before I tell of two occasions, very different in their sequel, in which the Lord was leading me, I will give my reader the view my father held on the urgency of getting right with God. Reference has been made to the earnest preaching of the gospel message in the days when he and my uncle worked as a team, but no undue pressure was used to bring people to the point of decision. I refer now to the days when Father preferred to give out the notices after the closing hymn, and well remember one occasion when he said this: "Our speaker this evening has spoken of the urgency that prevails concerning our soul's salvation, and has warned us of the uncertainty of life. This is very true, but I have another possibility in mind. At this moment, some may feel they need to get the matter settled; but by this time tomorrow that feeling may have gone, never to return!"

* * * * *

THE QUEST

No man, by searching, God can find,
For if he did, 'twould be his mind —
His intellect that played the part,
Conceived in head and not the heart.

If intellect is what's required —
That gift by men so much admired —
Then many could not make the grade
Through lack of that essential aid.

The physicist must clever be;
In splitting atoms he may see
God's wonderful creative Mind,
And yet not know this God so kind.

I know, thank God, there is a Way
Whereby the night is turned to day.
For in my quest for God to see,
God, in His grace, *has found out me.*

He put me in my place, 'tis true,
My need was to be "born anew".
It was my will, not just my mind
That needed change, I was to find.

My pride had made me shut the door;
I little cared that He who bore
Sin's penalty on Calvary
Was waiting by that door for me.

Tools of the Trade

> But God, in mercy, showed me then
> That Jesus died for careless men.
> So with repentance (change of mind),
> And faith in Christ, I peace did find.
>
> How true it is! God may be found,
> But not on intellectual ground.
> The heart that trusts Him knows full well
> That God with contrite hearts doth dwell.

* * * * *

The following experience that was mine will confirm this solemn truth:

Hearing that a man with whom we had done business for many years was dying, I felt a strong urge to visit him. Welcomed by his wife, I entered to find a very ill and weak man sitting at his card table. I then sought a way to tell him of the real purpose of my call, during which he leaned back in his chair, closed his eyes and listened. Suddenly, he broke in with something that had a true ring. "Jack," he said, "I am grateful for your concern but I must tell you that I am not interested, and I will give you my reason. When I was in my 'teens, there was a revival in religion, people were getting converted and I was taken up with it, up to a point; but life seemed to offer things I thought were more important, so I let it go. I want to tell you this, Jack: I'm not coming cringing to God now I'm dying; I'll take what comes."

Both he and his wife were warm in their thanks for my visit and I left the house deep in thought, wondering if this was a case of passing the 'point of no return'. I had worked on his cars for years before starting on my own and many a half-crown was pushed into my hand on completion of the job. Now I had something to offer a dying man, but he didn't want it. I was leaving him in God's hands; if he changed his mind and sought God's mercy he would have found it, but that was not for me to know. Unlike his son, who was killed in a motor accident some years later, he was certainly given time, and approached death with a clear mind. The case of the son was very different: his closing thoughts must have been how to pull up in time to avoid a tractor with trailer that was pulling over to the right as he was approaching at high speed. It had been a pleasure to do business with both men, but I am left with a sad reflection.

A few weeks later, and with this still fresh in my mind, a woman came into the office to see me personally. Her message was urgent: would I come down to see her husband, who was dying but unprepared? Needless to say, I was there almost as soon as this anxious wife, and again found a very sick man, but one who was wanting to get right with God. Real repentance was there, and so also was the Saviour of sinners, as the three of us were on our knees. I asked him to pray with me and ask forgiveness, which he readily did. To my surprise, his wife asked, "Can I give a little prayer?" The simplest of language being all that was needed, her cry ran:

> Gentle Jesus, meek and mild,
> Look upon a little child.
> Pity my simplicity,
> Suffer me to come to Thee.

There was joy in heaven that afternoon.

A few days later she came to thank me and said that she had never known him pray in all their married life. She added, "He is not the same man, he is kind to me!"

An evangelist friend, William Stevens, had been asked by Father to visit a dying man who lived not far from the Gospel Hall. Because the man was bitterly opposed to the Mission and all that it stood for, it was thought that the friend, being a stranger locally, might be allowed to see him; such proved to be the case, and I was present on his return. Though welcomed by the wife, he received a poor reception from the sick man; so much so that the friend went so far as to ask the man if he should tell the Lord that

Tools of the Trade

He wasn't wanted! This brought about a swift reaction which changed the situation dramatically. "No, no," he said, "Don'ee tell'm that!" Before he left the sick-room, he heard the sick man seek the mercy of God for forgiveness.

How different the departure of a believer with the knowledge of the Shepherd of Psalm 23! He is conscious that his Lord is near and has charge of all his affairs. There will be joy in the morning for him, and if his loved ones are in the good of all that Christ has done for them by His death on the cross, they too will look forward to the reunion.

A young man riding a motorcycle, with his wife and child in the sidecar, had pulled on to the forecourt and, seeing me standing by the office window, walked across to enquire about the let of my caravan that was standing in the field. Their problem was to find accommodation for twelve weeks, and not too far from his place of work. The builders had taken longer on their new bungalow than they had allowed for.

As the time for summer letting was near, and his cash being limited, I told him that I was sorry, but could not help him; but his look of disappointment, and that of his wife, as they talked together made me very unhappy. I had not made a note of his name, and he was now pulling away, but fortunately the traffic held them up and I was able to shout loud enough for him to hear, swing round, and learn of my reversed decision, and for me to learn his name — Clive Tomlinson.

Their gratitude for my change of heart was unbounded, and before the week was out a happy little family was installed in my caravan. Telling him a few days later about my change of mind, and Who was behind it, I found I was talking to a man deeply concerned about his soul. Convinced that the Lord was working in his heart, I gave him a copy of "The Reason Why", which he promised to read. It was no surprise to me when a short while later he came to tell me he was saved, and was full of joy. "It happened in church last Sunday morning. I don't think I was listening to the sermon; as I sat there I said to the Lord, 'Save me now'. And I knew He had done it and told my wife when I got home."

"And", he added, "her reaction was to tell me that she would be waiting to see how I behaved!"

A week or so later I challenged his wife, Sylvia, as to where she stood and was amazed with her reply. She said, "I gave my heart to Jesus at a camp when still in my 'teens, but the hostility of my parents shut my lips for good and all!" It was some while before she was restored to the Lord, and not without a hard struggle involving both of them. Several months later, I had a phone call telling me he had been baptised and was preaching the Gospel at every opportunity.

Many years later, as I listened to him preaching at Woodside Chapel, I recalled that it was on this very spot my caravan was standing when the Lord spoke to my conscience about my 'neighbour' being the man that needed my help!

I write some forty years after this incident and have learned that caution is advised in the use of the word 'saved' in describing conversion. To speak of our being saved will carry no weight if our behaviour pattern is out of line. It was indeed a happy day when "Jesus washed my sins away" and something to sing about. To be saved from hell is no small matter, but am I being saved from besetting sin, day by day?

It is my experience that only as I commit myself to being obedient to the Lord as He speaks to me, can I speak about being saved, or sing with any meaning:

Every day with Jesus is sweeter than the day before.
Every day with Jesus I'll praise Him more and more.
Jesus saves and keeps me, and He's the One I'm waiting for.
Every day with Jesus is sweeter than the day before.

Tools of the Trade

* * * * *

THE CHRISTIAN WORKSHOP

A workshop is built with a product in view.
We'll assume, for the moment, the worker is you.
This fact, from the start, should be well understood:
The job is worthwhile if the product is good.

In thinking of workshops we think too of tools.
To use them effectively there are set rules.
These rules don't in any way clash with God's grace.
Mishandling of tools can the product efface.

There must be right methods in how to proceed,
As well as right tools for meeting the need.
But, having all these, and with all things just so,
If the worker lacks love, there's nothing to show.

"Let no man despise thee because thou art young."
Thy faith and thy purity guarding the tongue,
To reading pay heed, or thy words will be thin.
You cannot give out if you fail to take in.

"Be thou an example to all that believe."
It may be thy manner of life will achieve
Far more than thy words, though important they be.
Remember, deportment is that which men see.

If we, in our working, go steadily on
With that which the Master assigns to His own,
And make it our aim to be faithful and true,
A glad day that will be, that day of review!

* * * * *

8: Under the Counter

It is common knowledge that the Motor Trade lends itself to dubious standards, the 'clocking' of speedometers being just one of the many ways in which people are taken in. Ingenious methods used to make the sale attractive are legion, but I refrain from enlarging for fear my reader may question the source from which I gain such knowledge!

About the time I started business on my own, I was shocked when passing a picture house where, across the front, was blazed "Ali Baba and the Forty Garage Proprietors"! I found myself asking if that was the hallmark of the business to which I had committed myself.

In fairness to my fellow traders and my own experience, I have often said there were more rogues outside our trade than within! Before I leave this picture which makes our lot look so grim, I have to say that the Trades Description Act does not apply to the harmless old lady who is parting with her pride and joy, but it does to me when I sell it!

The question might well be asked, "Can the Motor Trade be conducted by a Christian in a way that will not bring dishonour to the Lord?" My short answer is "Yes". But I am sure my reader will be asking how it's done, as did a fellow trader on one occasion!

We were on our way to a Vauxhall Dealers Meeting; he being at the wheel, and a steady driver, conversation was easy. Suddenly, with one eye on me and the other on the road, he fired a question that had obviously been kept in store: "Have all your deals been up to standard as a Christian, Jack?" He knew he would get a true answer, because rogues never lie to each other! For my part, I had no wish for it to be otherwise and I was very conscious that my Lord was listening.

I knew I was talking to a man who kept his selling staff hard at it but in no way would he tolerate low principles.

He was one of those concerned only to make money — the centre of discussion at these meetings. Without doubt, the Lord helped me in that conversation; in fact, the venue at Cheltenham appeared all too soon, and I looked forward to the journey home. But first a word about those Dealers Meetings.

In another context I would speak in similar vein of Fellowship Meetings (that is, convention-type meetings) where, at least at the superficial level, things were often discussed in much the same way! A more suitable description would be 'pep talks' because, generally speaking, the agenda would revolve around how to sell more cars and hold adequate stocks. Confidence in the goods being sold was all-important. (And, for the Christian, there is no use in speaking of the Lord Jesus Christ unless one has confidence in Him.) This would be followed by a 'talk-back', when various pressing issues would be ventilated. But before the session was over, the boys must be told to be good! A sample comes to mind.

"Have you done anything about all those dirty rags and junk under the benches, and did you get that workshop floor steam-cleaned and painted? You had it in your notes, gentlemen."

Oh yes, I did put it in my notes!

"What sort of chap have you got on your pumps? First impressions are important, you know."

I thought that was a good one for another occasion!

"When the family invade the showroom, don't overlook the small boy that opens every door and makes himself a nuisance, he may know more about cars than Dad. Put a sales gimmick in his hand and his chatter on the way home will put all thought of 'shopping around' out of mind; in fact, he may well sell that car for you!"

Of course, we didn't go to Cheltenham to listen to stuff we could have been given over the phone; I have picked out incidentals that were wedged in to vary the diet!

Subjects such as changes in design, market changes, stock control, all very ably presented, were the real matters that brought us together and, coming from such a wide area, all would come away with something; added to which there was the sharpening effect of like-minded people getting together.

For myself, however, I was leaving the hotel with a gasp for fresh air and praying for help in answering my friend's question in a way that would honour my Lord. I am sure he was given an insight into what Christ can be to the child of God, in dealing with his 'mess under the bench'! I noted that my friend spoke of Him as "The Architect of the Universe." I was speaking of One who died upon a cross, and when we parted we were of one mind that the day had been very profitable.

My greatest joy is to meet as often as possible with those who meet to consider everyday living in the light of eternity — although I have had good opportunities in speaking about the Lord at Dealers Meetings, and have one in mind: on this occasion the venue was Marlborough. It was my glass of soft drink which led this man to enquire the reason; to which I replied that observation had convinced me that, in working among young people, I could be of more help by steering clear of something that could lead them into trouble. It happened too often to ignore. His succession of questions about my activities seemed to indicate a background that might have been very revealing, had he thought to open up; but at the next meeting I was unable to catch his eye. Like my friend who questioned me about my deals, I have no doubt this man wondered how a person in the Motor Trade could live the Christian life and still stay in business!

My reader may be asking the same question, and the only answer I am able to give is that God put me there and kept me there, in spite of many bad falls. That is what this memoir is all about.

Back now to that pep talk, and first impressions being

important. It was not lost because, some months later, I found myself embarrassed by arriving late for a luncheon unconnected with my trade, but connected with Christian work. A seat just inside the door would have been very acceptable but, no, it had to be near the head of the table and in company with what appeared to be every minister in the area.

When the clapping had subsided (the applause being for my late arrival!) I thanked the gentleman responsible for the commotion — so unnecessary — and reminded him that the most inspiring person in his church was the man at the door who made it easier for the latecomer...! I would add that the lunch was good and the talk that followed very profitable. I find myself much more at home amongst a company of people who love the Lord, and who are concerned for those who are lost, and such was that occasion.

Some years ago I was being asked some pointed (if not awkward!) questions by a man working part-time in the office. Harry Hollister was not only a great help in getting some order into the books but, being a keen Christian of many years standing, gave me sound advice on spiritual things. I shall speak of him again in a different setting. My reaction on this occasion was to snap back at him, "Who are you working for, me or the Tax people?" He was not in the habit of economising on words, but my question made him swivel round on his stool, our eyes met, and he replied, "God". I got the message! In a competitive world, the problems facing the Christian are legion and the real test comes when he finds himself in a tight corner. The Fair Trading Act referred to will help to keep him from doing something that would land him in the courts, but will not help the bias in his nature when facing some of the finer decisions. Will he compromise? Unworthy standards in transactions rob us of all joy in our service for the Lord; we are unable to get clear, they stick and, if not dealt with, build up. To be pulled up by someone who feels he has had less than a right and proper deal is a humbling experience! I have found over the years that 'keeping short accounts with God' gives a peace of mind that enables one to think things through, and the courage to get it straight, cost what it may. If redress has to be made, our Lord will help us; but if, in His wisdom, no way is found as we would have wished, the truth remains: "Every one of us shall give account of himself to God" (2 Corinthians 5:10).

The message on the sundial —

"... the reckoning bideth".

Don Meadows, an old evangelist friend, once told me he found it helpful, as he left his bedroom, to hold the door handle for a moment before opening, to ask himself if all was well with that part of him that only his Lord could see! This reminds me of another, who told us he used Psalm 51 as the start for the day.

Over the past seventy years I have used the Scripture Union notes as a guide for daily reading, together with that marvellous collection of verses in the *Daily Light*, and found help; but perhaps it would have been more so had I given more thought to that door handle idea — together with an earlier setting of my alarm! Indeed, I would put it as vital to view our propensity to slackness as something needing definite action. We only get out what we put in, and we have the Lord's word for that:

"You will seek me and find me when you seek me with all your heart" (Jeremiah 29:13).

Peter experienced this and gives us sound advice:

"Be sober, be watchful: your adversary the devil, as a roaring lion, walks about, seeking whom he may devour" (1 Peter 5:8).

There are some things I still need to grapple with that may affect my day-to-day living. What folly it is to leave the door open when the lion is about! We do that when we open wide our eyes to see faults (or think we do) in other Christians. The practical relationship believers have

Under the Counter

with each other rests upon their relationship with the Lord, and in that sense it can be broken. He says, "You are my friends if you do the things I command you" (John 15:14). This should be borne in mind as we sing "What a Friend we have in Jesus". He is not only my Saviour and Keeper, He is also my Lord; but if I am to enjoy His friendship, and He mine, I must not lose sight of His holiness.

This is not just a Sunday exercise; I must take time to be holy. Time must be allotted not only for rest of the body but also for rest of the spirit, that part of me which enables me to worship and is part of my new birth. My reader may see these remarks tie up with what we have said about the two companies of people in which we often find ourselves.

I have often been asked if I ever have doubts about my salvation. For many years I have realised that my security lies in the work of Christ upon the cross, and so, while the short answer is "No", the tempter will still seek to seal my lips by enlarging on my failings.

The weapon used by the Lord in dealing with this foe in the wilderness was the Word of God, and what an armoury it is! God's promises are backed by the honour of His Name. I urge my reader to read and consider the last six verses of Hebrews 4: ". . . Jesus . . . was in all points tempted as we are, yet without sin". I find great comfort here: He understands me! We have no authority, nor is there any need, to seek the help of "saints" long since departed. I would say just here that if any of my sisters in Christ have a difficulty because Jesus is a man, they should consider this passage carefully, grasping its truth by faith. In doing so they will find rest in His love.

In my preamble I referred to the Lord finding it necessary to raise His voice at times; so now to the subject of chastisement: "My son, do not make light of the Lord's discipline, and do not lose heart when he rebukes you, because the Lord disciplines those he loves, and he punishes everyone he accepts as a son ... If you are not disciplined ... then you are illegitimate children and not true sons" (Hebrews 12:5-8).

A friend once told me he was startled when he heard an old man pray, "Thank you, Father, that you look upon us as sons, and not bastards." No doubt this man had done his homework and was now enjoying "... the peaceable fruits of righteousness" (Hebrews 12:11).

I had recently been asked if I thought a problem that had overtaken a fellow believer was the chastening hand of the Lord in correction, and I am glad the noise of the car hindered my reply for a while! Our judgment in such matters can easily be hasty, shallow and somewhat harsh, whereas caution is needed and time to think before venturing any comment.

I revere the memory of the way my father handled my correction, but he was fallible. My Father in heaven makes no mistakes, His ways are perfect. If I resist His chastening, you will find me low indeed; but submissiveness to His loving correctives will always bring peace and joy. I can well afford to withhold judgment on my brother's need, in this respect, paying more heed to my own!

A missionary who, with his wife, was about to return to the Far East, having reached the difficult decision to leave their three children behind, said in my hearing, "Please, our need is for your prayers, not your censure!" Fault-finding is all too easy and can become a habit that dies hard. A remedy always to hand is to seek reasons for words of encouragement!

I have a feeling that an old employee reading this will be saying, "It's a pity the Governor didn't come in on this one a bit earlier!"

A discussion took place in the office with a man working part-time on my books; this was just after the war and the conversation drifted to the world situation. He was a very astute person and had risen quite high before retirement. He also had some standing in his

Lodge, but I gathered from what he told me that his home life was another matter! "We've got to get back to the Sermon on the Mount", was his comment, but he could offer no clue as to where ability to carry out these high principles could be found!

Some months after he left me, I received news that he was terminally ill in a nursing home, which prompted me to visit him without delay. He had gone for a short walk when I arrived but I was directed to where I could find him. I soon picked up a sick and lonely man who was so pleased to see me; indeed, it was not long before he unburdened his heart. Almost his first words were, "I've been a rotter!" His mind was clear as we sat and talked in the car, not about the Sermon on the Mount now, but about the Lord Jesus Himself, and what He had done for poor sinners like the pair of us.

For me, it was deeply moving to hear him pray for forgiveness in terms I have used myself. I saw him only once after that occasion, and in a different nursing home. He told me how thankful he was that we chatted that day and that he was now ready to meet the Lord.

The service at the crematorium, a week or so later, was very dignified and much was said about his activities as a Mason, but I came away with other thoughts, and a heart full of thankfulness to God that my friend had sought mercy, and was now with the Lord he had so lately found.

It is a cause of concern that so many with whom one is in contact are nice people, both to know and do business with, but do not appear to have any interest in the things of God. In fact, to speak of the Lord Jesus in a personal way can be to lose their friendship, and yet they are the very people we long to win for Christ.

We are often put to shame by the high ethical standards of people who rest on these for acceptance with God and who are offended if you point out their error on this subject. Not that I ever did in the case I now relate. I am thinking of a high-ranking Army officer in retirement, who always insisted on 'getting it right'. It was war-time, and he applied for one gallon of petrol a month to cover a weekly journey of six miles with a 16 horse power car, and was not, he said, asking or allowing me to help from 'under the counter'! This was something for me to ponder! When he was very ill, I gave him a copy of the S.G.M. booklet "Words of Comfort". On my last visit he told me that he had always thought keeping the commandments was sufficient in being right with God, but now realised his mistake.

A few weeks after his death his widow showed me the little book, now scarcely legible, and told me he would read nothing else. I have no doubt the Spirit of God used the Scriptures to open his eyes, and he died resting on the work of the Lord Jesus alone.

Since my days in Parkstone, I have always been fascinated with bees, having watched an expert hiving a swarm in a neighbour's garden. He wore a veil but no gloves, and to expedite things he gently helped the little creatures with bare hands. Having bought a new hive, and placed it on the heather at West Moors, I awaited the promised swarm. It was brought in a cardboard box and placed on the workshop floor with, "Here's your bees, Jack!"

That evening, with veil but no gloves, I emptied the cardboard box on to the carefully prepared run-up, the bees flowing like liquid over the board. It wasn't long before the queen, riding rough-shod on the backs of her subjects, made her way through the entrance. Then, from all directions, the bees followed, needing no assistance — or did they? . . . It was just then I was to learn a lesson in bee-keeping that was to come home to me about soul-winning! I leave my reader to picture the young man in obvious distress as he distances himself from that hive, and his difficulty in handling his tools the next morning! Did it put me off? By no means! Bee-keeping really holds you, and before I leave the subject I would go back to that "mess under the bench".

The well-ordered society of bees allows no dirt whatever in the hive. On more than one occasion I had qualms of conscience when, due to laziness (or was it meanness?), I gave a new swarm some dirty old combs in which to store their nectar! The following morning would reveal a pile of rubbish below the entrance, and, if examined, those combs would be spotless.

The writer of Proverbs 6:6 evidently didn't keep bees, but he got the same message from the ant. I still need reminding! "Go to the ant, you sluggard; consider its ways and be wise! It has no commander, no overseer or ruler, yet it stores its provisions in summer and gathers its food at harvest."

9: Over the Counter

A question I have often asked myself is: what impression do I convey to the people I contact as to the kind of a person God is, whom I seek to follow? For many are of the opinion that the life of a Christian must be one of gloom, brought about by renunciations and restrictions — as though God wants to deprive us in some way!

Whether or not I contribute to this falsity, the truth is that our lives would be empty without Him. True believers are of one mind about this. Maybe a 'one track mind', but I'm glad to be one of their number!

Recently, a friend of many years' standing, Dick White, lost his wife suddenly; this followed the death of their only son a few years previously. Farming in a fairly big way, their home was always open to those in need, and where the meeting held each month for the villagers was such that if you arrived late you had to sit half-way up the stairs. The funeral service held in the Chapel was, for me, a time of real spiritual enrichment, as no doubt it was for many others. When later I shared this with the dear man in his time of sorrow, he declared, "Jack, we've got something the unbeliever knows nothing about!" A Christian *overcome* with grief can provide a handle for unbelievers to reject Christ. Since that conversation, our brother has lost his son-in-law through an accident on his farm.

* * * * *

SAFELY ANCHORED

God's judgments are unsearchable,
His ways past finding out.
His matters are inscrutable,
Of none gives He account.

It seems that many dare to think
Our God is someone small!
They careless live, till on the brink
Of death before they call.

Over the Counter

But call they must, upon the Lord
If they His saved would be.
God ever has the final word
On mankind's destiny.

For those that on the Lord do call
Receive salvation free,
And owning Christ as Lord of all
Find glorious liberty.

Christ's riches are unsearchable.
His tried ones oft have proved
Though hot may be the crucible,
Faith stands — serene — unmoved.

Their God is big, His power is strong,
No figment of the mind.
They know Him, — love Him, — and they long
To be as gold, refined.

Steep paths they oft are called to tread
With blind and narrow bend.
It is through these they're gently led
By Him who's now their friend.

They know full well that "God is Love"
And "perfect is His way".
The "Whys" they leave to Him above,
And satisfied are they.

* * * * *

A line my Mother often quoted ran, "Not a single shaft can hit, till the God of love sees fit", and those who are anchored say, "Amen". Psalm 94:18-19 reads:

*When I said, My foot slippeth;
thy mercy, O LORD, held me up.
In the multitude of my thoughts within me
thy comforts delight my soul."*

This was quoted in a letter from Mr Harold Barker in the early days of the war — a man who had just lost twelve members of his family by a torpedo attack in the Channel. His son, Eric (a missionary in Portugal), whom I knew well, had been advised to send his wife and seven children, also her sister and her family, back from Portugal to the U.K. while he stayed to continue the gospel campaign — they all lost their lives in this attack. In the aftermath of the tragedy the Lord saw fit to bless Eric's ministry in a remarkable way, which, since his upbringing was very similar to mine, has given me cause to ponder these things and seriously reflect upon them. How thankful I am that the truths of Scripture I was taught in my formative years were basic to everyday living!

In my early years I continually listened to the Scriptures being expounded. *Redemption, regeneration, justification, sanctification* were all familiar words, but they were to take on new meaning when, as a teenager, I surrendered to the Lordship of Christ. The point I make here is, that as my knowledge increased, so also did my responsibility to apply them by faith to my everyday life, as I did when I sought God's mercy in the first place. Taking them in the order given above:

Redemption: He bought me; I belong to Him.
Regeneration: He imparted His life to me. I was dead.
Justification: He acquitted me. I was guilty.
Sanctification: He made me holy. I was unclean.

Christ's death on the cross alone has brought about my new standing before God. I ask my reader, "Is the tale worth telling?"

Sowing Seeds

Now back to my job for a moment, and the problem of living the Christian life in today's world. Being self-employed, the wise use of my time needed much thought. Before new vehicles arrived on transporters, I found the job of going to London and then Luton by train to collect a new vehicle helped me considerably, because I was alone for most of the day, and often those hours were spent in communion with my Lord and I came home refreshed in spirit.

A verse I found helpful when encouragement was sorely needed runs: "In the morning sow thy seed, and in the evening withhold not thine hand: for thou knowest not whether shall prosper, either this or that, or whether they both shall be alike good" (Ecclesiastes 11:6).

* * * * *

THE SOWER

Eyes upon your Lord and Master,
Hearken to His loving call.
Feet well shod for running faster,
Praying to avoid a fall.
Use your voice to sing His praises,
Talents must be used for Him.
Walking in the Light, witness ever bright,
Never losing sight . . . of Jesus.

Working for your Lord and Master,
He will give you seed to sow.
Whether this or that may prosper,
Spread it as you onward go.
Well prepare the ground for sowing,
Hearts are often hard and sad.
When they see we care, problems they will share,
We can speak just there . . . of Jesus.

Soon the scene will change to glory,
So we plough and sow in hope.
Labour is the earthly story
Ending on a heavenly note.
All because the Lord of harvest
Died to give us precious seed!
He alone doth know how the seed will grow
When we speak below . . . of Jesus.

* * * * *

I have often looked into the faces of a handful of children before me — full of attention one Sunday but seemingly a waste of my time the next — and would reason that the cause must be 'fish for breakfast' or 'they break up tomorrow'; but could never get clear of where the *real* reason might lie, knowing in my heart that whatever excuses I might put forward for their inattentiveness, my lack of preparedness was the cause, and my guilty conscience niggled me. I ask the Lord to make the seed grow; but the conditions for growth must be right if there is to be a harvest. Looking back, I regret not giving more time and thought to this important work — I am thinking of occasions when I hung on too long in the office on a week night, dashing off immediately after work to pick up the children, and then trying to hold their attention on an empty stomach!

I now realise the Lord has been very gracious to me, and I am humbled before Him, as years later one of these children, perhaps a Mum or Dad, tells me the claims of the Lord Jesus were first made clear to them in my class.

I once found myself sitting by the bedside in the hospital, where a man of about my own age, George Cockwell, lay terminally ill; his family were all there and he was ready to leave them. We spoke of the days when, as a lad in his 'teens, he attended the Gospel Tent Mission at Herston, and where the seed sown had not been lost —

Father was having some trouble with this boy showing off, which led him to put the offender in his place for that meeting! The following morning, this great big lad came banging on the door of the caravan, demanding an interview.

"I'm going to fight you for making me look small in front of the others!"

Feeling himself to be no match for this overgrown schoolboy, Father realised a 'punch-up' was out of the question; other tactics must be employed — and he was a very resourceful man.

"Yes, George, I'll come down and fight you; but, before I do, I must tell you that I have never lost a fight yet, and won't this one."

"We'll see about that. You come down and I'll show you!" said George.

After repeating the warning, Father noted a slight change in tone indicating a chink in George's bravado which should be exploited. So, after another warning, George is invited to do the sensible thing and come up into the caravan to discuss the issue.

A lengthy talk it was, perhaps with the necessary refreshments, but it ended with Father having his usual last word! —

"Who has won the fight, then, George?"

They were friends for life, and I don't know when it was that George found the Saviour, but the man I visited in Poole hospital knew where he was going, and why.

We don't know which 'shall prosper', but there will be a harvest.

Still on the subject of 'sowing', I must again bring in my Grandma Foley with the broken hip. Before being confined to bed, and realising time was short, she made her daily walk (aided by two sticks) an occasion for witnessing; and before setting out, would pray that the seed, if planted, would grow.

A lady is working in her garden that adjoins the road and, Grandma being a keen gardener herself, the conversation gets off to a good start, and then quickly takes a turn to the all-important subject.

"I've been wanting to know if you love the Lord Jesus?"

"Oh yes, Mrs Foley, I do."

"I am glad, because I am sure you will be reading your Bible, and worshipping with God's people!"

Grandma Foley was a remarkable woman and lived to the age of 99; a keen student of prophecy, with a mind clear to the end. Her daughter, Annie, only twenty years younger and full of rheumatism, gave her devoted love and care, rejecting marriage in order to do so. On occasions, she heard Grandma scolding the Lord (if that is the right word!), "Lord, don't wait until I am pure gold, take me home now!"

I am glad to say that, before she took to her bed, she had the joy of seeing Uncle John, now completely restored, partaking at the Lord's Table. Indeed, it was a joy to us all, especially to his brother.

I have often had cause to reflect, as I browse through books acquired over the years, many from which Grandma would sometimes quote, that although I have been enriched by reading, it was not to the extent of my forebears; mine has been too cursory. If the material was good, they were not satisfied with quick reference, they applied themselves to the subject. Their reading was never just killing time. Father told me that I lacked 'stickability'; another word he used was 'grit'. It was clear where he got his supply, but I often wished he had passed a bit more on to me! He would say, "You are losing your way, Son, by not spending enough time with your Bible!" I must confess his comment was too near the bone for my comfort; he will be back again before I finish my story, but a word here about his sister.

When I was young, Aunt Annie helped me with my reading, and later, when I started working in Parkstone, I lodged for a while in her home. Tall, vivacious, but very Victorian, she had a sweet bewitching smile that 'got you' at times; I was very fond of her, although she was 'one too many' for me at times, as I will explain. My temper had got the better of me and I was expressing myself somewhat 'ill-advisedly' with my lips. Drawing herself up above full height, and moving closer to me with eyes flashing, she felled me with, "Sir, how dare you!" It was really an advance on Mother's mouth wash and I assure my reader that it worked.

I now go to Mother's side of the family, and my grandmother in particular, who lived all her life in Edinburgh.

Over the Counter

On the death of her husband, Grandma Scott was left with a young family of six. Handicapped by poor eyesight, and fully aware that total blindness lay ahead, she made the Bible her only reading; prayer was the very air she breathed; and the Psalms she would quote by heart.

"Sir, how dare you!"

I have often heard Father speak of Alec, one of her four sons, as being a great help at the time of his conversion — and doubtless Alec's sister Margaret did her bit! But it's Grandma I have in mind. Before the Foleys left Edinburgh for Bristol, my guess is that the grandmothers Scott and Foley had much in common!

Grandma Scott's second son, Mother's brother Andrew, left home for Australia in the hope of making a living by fruit farming, but this eluded him and he went bankrupt. After a few years all contact with those at home was lost. I know that Mother thought he was no longer alive, but both she and his mother firmly believed they would meet him in heaven, as he was the burden of their prayers. How right they were!

I was aware of all this, and many years after their deaths I received a letter from Uncle Andrew, aged over eighty and quite blind, telling me he had recently been saved, all by the mercy of God. This moved me deeply and I replied at once. Then, a few months later, I received a letter from a Baptist minister to inform me that Uncle had died peacefully. "Scottie", he said, "was my first convert when I came to Australia."

My reader will appreciate that these records of simple, child-like faith are embedded in my mind. To them, in a measure, I can add my own experience. Prayer is the privilege of being able to touch the throne of Almighty God, and this thought takes me back again, to the last two years of school holidays which were spent with my Uncle John in Worth Matravers, where he had set up several railway carriages as dwellings.

He was as keen on fishing as I was, and the two of us, armed with makeshift rod and line, with a hard but delicious sago pudding in a bag that, hopefully, would later carry smelly fish, would spend many happy hours on the rocks at Seacombe or Dancing Ledge.

These holidays were full of variety because Uncle had given me a small dinghy, which in the summer months I kept near Swanage pier. The incident that follows took place at Seacombe Quarries, on the edge of the cliffs.

The cottage overlooked the sea, a mile distant, and if in the morning one could see the little puffs of white foam, Uncle would say, "No fishing today, the dogs are out — too dangerous". It so happened that on one lovely calm day I was not going to have his company and therefore anticipated a freedom that was rare. We seldom fished from the outer ledge because even on a calm day the swell could be treacherous, but we used a wide fissure in the rocks that on hot days I found very inviting. However, in no way was I allowed to bathe there because of the problem of getting out, the sides being almost vertical most of the way round. Today I was full of ideas, and whilst I don't recall misgivings due to warnings given, I know my knowledge of the Bible often gave me a twinge! The verse that gave me much disquiet ran: "He, that being often reproved hardeneth his neck, shall suddenly be destroyed, and that without remedy" (Proverbs 29:1). Even sound advice seemed to have no relevance just then as I made my way, ostensibly to fish, but with bathing suit in bag! Running most of the way, and in faster time than it takes to bait a hook, the long-awaited plunge was made! I had been taught that the Bible word "repentance" means "to change one's mind" — and for me this must have been the fastest change ever! The water was numbingly cold, and so my next move was clear. The moments that followed were unforgettable. The baths at school were fitted with a rail to hold, but here the long wet seaweed just mocked me as I grabbed it and fell back into deep water.

Fully aware that I was alone and that shouting was useless, I was very frightened. There must have been moments of reflection, but what I now know is that my plight was seen by the One who controls the ocean's ebb and flow, and the swell that so often has its danger was His provision for lifting me above the seaweed, allowing me something to hold on to and scramble to safety. Cuts on arms and legs there were, but I was alive! It was a painful walk back to the cottage, but God in His mercy had been speaking to me once again.

I don't remember the explanation of events that day, but I must have given Uncle some kind of tale that averted his wrath. Maybe he was only too thankful to know I was safe. However, I know the truth came out later.

One Sunday morning found us in the Methodist chapel where, sitting on the front row, was an elderly man whom I had often seen in the village, and who now was about to take the opening prayer. Slowly rising to his feet, and with his back to the congregation, he started to pray in a voice that reminded me of the fog warning at Portland! It was not unlike Uncle's voice but was set in a lower key; the difference being that, as he proceeded, the volume and pitch rose in what seemed a never-ending scale, until the roof timbers said, "Enough!" — or I thought they did! On the way home I broke the pensive silence by remarking on this extraordinary prayer:

"Why does a man pray like that?"

"Ah, my boy, that is what we call 'praying with unction'."

At the time I was not aware of the reason why Uncle was no longer preaching. As I look back now on that incident, I am sure my remark set his mind back to the days when prayer, however expressed, was vital to him, and perhaps that accounted for his reflective mood.

I often saw the old man sitting outside his cottage near the village pub and was told that at one time he had been a Methodist local preacher — one of a number left high and dry and very disturbed with the new "modernistic" teaching that had spread from the Continent and was being widely accepted in this country. These godly men had firmly held the Bible to be the Word of God, but the modern thought held the Scriptures merely to 'contain' the word of God. It then explained away the miracles, the virgin birth and the resurrection of Christ, leaving faith with nothing to rest upon, and without which "it is impossible to please God" (Hebrews 11:6).

Behind these denials lies the rejection of the truth that Jesus died an atoning death. In all, this is a teaching that does nothing to help man in his deepest need, and many fall for it because it does not touch the conscience. It views Christ as a martyr, placing Him on the same level as themselves.

As in Paul's day, men still make 'merchandise' of the Word of God and, because of this (to take a present-day example), some earnest Christians feel they must drop the expression "born again" as it is being used by spurious so-called evangelists. But is this not playing into the hands of these modern false teachers? We ought not to be ashamed to use the words of Jesus on such an important issue. He says to Nicodemus: "Except a man be born again, he cannot see the kingdom of God" (John 3:3).

To be "born again" — or, alternatively, "born from above" — is regeneration, not reformation, and both Paul and John (and also Peter) have much to say on this new birth. They also tell us how these people that huckster the Word of God should be treated. They must be given no quarter whatever, says John in 2 John 10. Elsewhere in my story I have referred to some of my friends (for example, Brigadier General Frost) who have had no inhibitions about exposing those who deceive, and they probably had good reasons for doing so! The Lord Jesus was moved to do this on occasions, as for example in his exposure of the Pharisees in John 8:44, but His purpose in coming was to seek and to save that which was lost.

As Father and Uncle were covering the villages with the gospel, they were repeatedly told by the older folk, "We haven't heard this for years", and their joy was unbounded. An elderly man, Mr Chinchin by name, a baker in Langton Matravers, was so thrilled by hearing a clear presentation of the gospel that he brought a huge bread and butter pudding, at a time when Father had three hungry fellows with him, plus the writer on school holiday. I remember it well because one of these men loathed bread and butter puddings. Father saw to it that he stayed hungry! Many years later, a much wiser man, home on furlough from the mission field, he had obviously learned a lesson I had mastered as a boy!

This brings me to a point that I would wish to clarify, because people are sometimes puzzled by what seems to them a far too cock-sure position taken by Christians concerning eternal security. The fact is that people who mess around with the Word of God have no assurance of salvation because they have taken away the basis on which assurance rests.

While his car was being serviced I was chatting to a minister one day when this subject of assurance arose, being one that lay close to my heart. I was in for a surprise, because when I made reference to Paul's letter to the church in Rome he told me he found it so difficult he wished Paul had never written it! I knew him to be a man of prayer and devoted to his work, but the poor fellow had no assurance whatever, and I grieved for him. Some years later, however, long after he retired, I visited him in hospital and had no need to enquire then about his view of *Romans*: God's truth had sunk deeper; he was anchored.

Looking back, I am glad Father valued *Romans* in the way he did. So much so that when I stayed with him on Blandford Camp, we read *Romans* every morning. I may not have understood it then, but, thanks to Dad, I got the words and they stuck! The teaching is basic, and if my reader is patient, I will try to outline that masterpiece as I understand it.

It is all about a holy God acquitting a guilty man and giving him a new standing on a righteous basis. Only a loving God would plan to do this, or could. Man's need as

Over the Counter

a sinner is very clear and he is helpless to do anything about it. However, God does give him (if he is willing to receive it) the capacity to place his faith in God's mercy to save him from sin's consequences. Faith is the only key God recognises in this important matter and He will allow no other. By its very nature, faith must have an object, and it was God's love for man, in his wretched and hopeless state, that moved Him to send His Son into the world to deal with this problem that separates man from God. Man is unable to save himself, God alone must do it, and He does it through Jesus. Faith in Jesus is to believe His claims and rely on what He has done by His death and resurrection.

By His death on the cross, the sinless Son of God has taken the place of the guilty man who has sought God's mercy. That man will no longer face eternal death (separation from God); he has been justified (cleared of every charge). But it will not be long before he faces the problem of not being what his conscience tells him he should be. This did not trouble him before, but it does now, and Paul indicates (chapter 7) that he knows what he is talking about.

However, in chapter 8 he makes it abundantly clear that victory is his through the indwelling Spirit. Faith again is needed, and this leads him to see that God has given him a new life and views him in a new light. He has adopted him into His family as a son. Satan can do his worst (and he will try), but this man is secure. Jesus is alive and will keep him from sinning as his faith leads him to obey.

It need not surprise us that the devil will seek to discredit the truth of the resurrection of Him who "was raised again for our justification" (Romans 4:25).

Someone has said, "The assurance of salvation is the root and soil of holiness". Paul, in chapter 12, tells us what is expected of the man, now that he has been acquitted in God's court of justice and enters his court of worship. In another letter, he says: "Old things are passed away . . . all things are become new" (2 Corinthians 5:17). I feel I must enlarge on this.

Because the believer is now indwelt by the Holy Spirit, he finds many of the former pleasures very hollow. The borderline joke, for example, is now unacceptable. The position is clear, but our minds are not a vacuum: something has to take the place of what is discarded. We are what we feed upon.

* * * * *

ON DIET

A simple lesson for our good
Suggested by our choice of food
May prove (if giv'n due thought) to be
A suitable analogy.

We choose the foods we think are nice,
And for our choice we pay the price.
But only when our ship's "off course"
Give careful thought about their source.

Then time, oft scarce for taking food
In truth is ours in plenitude.
We see, at last, the need to pay
Due heed in choice of food each day.

Thus, feeding needs to be controlled;
For this, each one, a key doth hold.
With power the television strives
And makes fair bid to shape our lives.

The world, with food for eye and heart
Appeals to man in every part.
Its aim is clear beyond all doubt.
Its sin is that it leaves God out.

But faith in Christ doth bring God in,
For at the Cross we may begin
To walk a path where we are fed
By Him Who is the Living Bread.

Over the Counter

With heart so big, the world's too small,
None less than Christ can fill our all.
He waits to do just that (what grace!),
Make hearts like ours His dwelling place!

* * * * *

Hungry souls there are, that find and eat
God's manna day by day —
And glad they are, their life is fresh and sweet,
For as their food are they.

(G. T. Steegen)

As never before, voices from the business world are yelling, "Get on or get out!" Such are the all-consuming demands of business life that business tries to own the man, whereas the Christian is under Christ's ownership. My Lord whispers, "Them that honour Me, I will honour." We honour Him by allowing Him His place in our thinking, which is where it all starts. Our thought life is the seed-bed of all our actions. In this connection it was Solomon who said: "For as he thinketh in his heart, so is he" (Proverbs 23:7). This being so, our head needs protection.

Whilst driving recently through the pleasant Purbeck countryside, we saw a large notice which had been erected by an oil drilling concern which read: "Helmets must be worn in this area." It brought to mind Paul's warning to the church in Ephesus concerning the "fiery darts of the wicked", urging his readers to "take the helmet of salvation", along with the "sword of the Spirit, which is the word of God" (Ephesians 6:13-18); also the Psalmist: "Thy word have I hid in my heart, that I might not sin against Thee" (Psalm 119:11).

Paul concludes his words on the Christian's warfare by pressing the importance of prayer and adding, when we pray, to be sure to remember him! My reader will, no doubt, have gathered that I share those sentiments!

I have drifted somewhat, as Paul has done, from justification to the closely related subject of sanctification; so back to the man who has been acquitted in God's court of justice and finds himself in His court of worship. His heart is full of thankfulness to God who is no longer his enemy, because Christ has become his Substitute, and lives to keep him secure. It is mercy from first to last and so, in chapter 12, Paul says to this man, and his readers: "I beseech you therefore, brethren, by the mercies of God, that you present your bodies a living sacrifice, holy, acceptable unto God, which is your reasonable service. And be not conformed to this world: but be transformed by the renewing of your mind, that you may prove what is that good, and acceptable, and perfect, will of God" (Romans 12:1,2).

I am told the word 'reasonable' means 'intelligent'. This thought is expanded in verse 2, where a transformation takes place in the mind. If this man has "presented his body" as a "living sacrifice" — that is to say, he had committed himself 'in toto' to his new Owner — he is going to face problems in every area of his life; for which his mind must be clear in seeing his duty to his neighbours, friends, enemies, fellow Christians, civil authorities — the lot! I wish I had grasped this more fully sixty years ago!

The question may be asked, "Must a dying man, on the brink of eternity, grasp all this doctrine in order to be right with God?" Two scriptures come to mind that will help us here. The first is found in Acts 16 and is that of the jailer in Philippi. Faced with certain execution for failing in his duty, and quite unprepared for death, he cries, "What must I do to be saved?" The answer is clear and direct: "Believe on the Lord Jesus Christ and you shall be saved." He did just that, and found peace.

The second is told by Jesus Himself, and is found in Luke 18. It is about two men who went into the temple to pray. One was a publican, the other a Pharisee. The latter

Over the Counter

thanks God that he is better than all other men, or even "this publican", and then lists his achievements, both negative and positive, and in that order! The publican takes his place as a sinner and seeks God's mercy, and Jesus says of him (v.14): "This man went down to his house justified, rather than the other." A solemn indictment!

* * * * *

THE TWO PRAYERS

A well-respected man it was
That visited God's house that day:
The Pharisee was there because
It was the thing to do — to pray.

But Someone else was standing by,
And listened as each spoke in prayer.
He knew the history — heard each sigh
Of every heart that gathered there.

One prayer He heard did run like this,
"I do ... I don't ... I tithe ... I fast —
In fact there's nothing far amiss
That makes me now regret the past."

This code of ethics was the theme
He dared recite before God's throne!
Of highest order, it would seem —
Yet coming from a heart of stone.

But one, reflecting in the dark,
Thought to himself, "That sounded fine!
Is that the prayer that God doth mark?
For that experience is not mine.

I come because I feel my need,
And this my opportunity.
I've sinned in thought, and word, and deed,
O God, be merciful to me."

> That sin is "just to miss the mark",
> The Pharisee had failed to learn.
> Persistent pride is to embark
> Upon a path of no return.
>
> The tax collector peace did find,
> As homeward wended he his way.
> A load was gone from heart and mind,
> For "justified" was he that day.

* * * * *

Returning to the question, a dying man would hardly be able to grasp doctrine, but, if he is conscious of his need, he can call for mercy and will find it. For, as the apostle says in Romans 10:9, "If thou shalt confess with thy mouth the Lord Jesus, and shalt believe in thine heart that God hath raised him from the dead, thou shalt be saved"; and again in v.13: "For whosoever shall call upon the name of the Lord shall be saved". And if he lacks assurance, the words of Jesus to the dying thief should bring peace to his heart. I quote again from Romans 5:8: "God commendeth His love toward us, in that, while we were yet sinners, Christ died for us." And again, in Romans 8:1: "There is now therefore no condemnation to them that are in Christ Jesus."

This is what takes place when God "justifies the ungodly". He not only forgives his sins, He also credits the repentant sinner with His own righteousness. Grasping this truth removes any doubts we may have about our security. The hymn puts it very well:

> *When Satan tempts me to despair,*
> *And tells me of the guilt within,*
> *Upward I look, and see Him there*
> *Who made an end to all my sin.*

Whilst we deplore it, as Christians we are often overcome by sin, and, if it is not confessed and forgiven, we shall have to face it when we stand before the

Over the Counter

"judgment seat of Christ" (2 Corinthians 5:10). This judgment seat is not to be confused with the "great white throne" of Revelation 20:11, before which the ungodly will stand. The believer has been delivered from that, through Christ's death on his behalf, praise God! But the tribunal, which is what this judgment seat is, will be the occasion when those who have been faithful to their Lord will be rewarded; nothing will be overlooked. All that has been confessed and forgiven will not be brought to light; it has been covered by the Blood (1 John 1:7-9); but the careless believer will suffer loss.

This reference to the apostle John's first Epistle leads me to enlarge, because it follows Paul's teaching on justification and speaks of the way it should affect our everyday lives.

It is not clear how much personal contact these apostles had with each other, but they both make it plain they had personal contact with the risen Christ. John's view in this letter is that God is light, and God is love.

I have referred earlier to friends of mine who have passed through times of grief and have not only been preserved from a morbid self-indulgence in sorrow, but have found in it a comfort that is positive because of their relationship with God. John uses the word "fellowship" (1 John 1:3). If this letter is read through at a sitting it will be noticed that the writer is concerned that his readers get their relationships right — and, I might say, in three directions — with the triune God, with fellow Christians, and with the world. This is something the Christian has to do for himself, as John makes clear at the close of the letter. This is the secret for the "boldness" or "confidence" that he mentions several times, and will go a long way to avoiding a setback when the wind of adversity blows.

Once, when on holiday in the Midlands, we attended the morning service in the village chapel of Milton-under-Wychwood and were privileged to hear a clear gospel message. In thanking the minister, I remarked on his liberty in this respect and received this comment in reply: "I have no problem in preaching the gospel of salvation whatever, but if I get onto the subject of personal sanctification, I am in trouble. Many make it clear they do not want to hear it!" What he was getting at is that the matter of personal, daily reformation is too close to the bone for some! I had found the same, and it is sad, and I hasten to add there was a time when I was in the same state of heart and my Lord, in His mercy, pressed it home to my conscience. Accepting its truth, my joy in the Lord was restored. The following scriptures are relevant here: John 5:22,27; Romans 14:10; 2 Corinthians 5:10.

* * * * *

LOYALTY

Lord, my heart runs after Thee.
Joyful when Thou leadest me,
Over paths to me unknown,
There converse with Thee alone,
Conscious of Thy kindness shown
    Lord Jesus.

Lord, my joy in Thee is full,
Even though I feel the pull
Of a world that has no time
For a Saviour such as mine,
Or a subject so sublime
    Lord Jesus.

Lord, like Thee I long to grow;
In this grace I've far to go.
Help me, Lord, to always shine;
Fill with love, Thy love divine;
Daily life resembling Thine
    Lord Jesus.

Lord, afresh my spirit keen,
So that things that come between
Thee and me I put away,

Over the Counter

> Give more time to watch and pray,
> As I wait Your "Coming" day
> Lord Jesus.

* * * * *

When the Lord was with His disciples in the Upper Room, He was aware they would have problems in their relationship with each other when He left them. Harmony was vital if their witness was to be effective in the world. His words are clear: He says, "A new commandment I give unto you, that you love one another; as I have loved you, that you also love one another. By this shall all men know that you are My disciples, if you have love one to another" (John 13:34-35).

I once heard this subject pressed with some vigour, and as we were leaving the meeting, the organist turned to me with, "We love each other when we don't see too much of each other, don't we?" My reply to this lady I thankfully have forgotten but, over the years, we both have grown, and the message was not lost!

"Get things right on this side of life, Son, or you will have to put them right on the other!" This was said to me by my Father more than once and the incident that follows will illustrate his views on the subject; for me, the episode was unforgettable, and goes back to the time before I was married.

I arrived for the midday meal to find Father at issue with another elder of the church. They loved each other well and were both strong-minded men who held the Lord's honour to be paramount in their service for Him. I had witnessed Father's anger often, having been its cause more often than not, but that of this elder was new to me and somewhat disturbing — though he told me once that his hair used to be red! I was never told the reason for the upset, but at the moment we have two angry men parting with hot words, and overheard by Mother in the kitchen, and by me.

As the three of us are sitting down to a silent lunch, the door opens. Father rises to his feet; no words are spoken but two men, with eyes streaming and arms around each other, are getting things put right. I went back to work that afternoon feeling that I had been in the sanctuary! In situations like this, someone has to make the first move; I need the grace of God to be that one! Neither of these men would have taken of the Lord's Supper with that hanging over them; both would have felt a responsibility to the Lord's people as they worshipped, being inseparably bound together as the "body of Christ". The Holy Spirit will be very sensitive to any disunity, this being a complete negation of the purpose and meaning of the Lord's Table. Love expressing itself in forgiveness is essential to the restoration of unity.

I have drawn attention to the Lord's words to his disciples on the subject of love toward each other, as recorded by John at the end of his long life. He says nothing about the institution of the Supper — this had been done by others. However, with remarkable clarity, he enlarges on the Lord's teaching on that occasion, including His prayer to His Father in which He sums up with these words: "Holy Father, keep them in Thy Name ... that they may be one, even as we are" (John 17:11).

This important subject often surfaced with Father's helpers at Swanage whose future would involve working with others — Eric Bermejo (later to serve in Spain), Reg Barnes, Sidney Lawes and Wilf Durham (who both went to India), and Frank Herring who was a keen open air speaker and for a time Father's chief helper until marriage took him to Dorchester where he brought into being the Arts and Crafts Shop. Prison work was his special calling in his service for the Lord. Without doubt Father's insight made impact of lasting benefit on many who are no longer with us but whose "works follow them" (Revelation 14:13).

* * * * *

EPISCOPY

Unto yourselves take heed,
And to the flock of God.
The Church whom you should feed
Was purchased with His blood.
No "lording" o'er your charge,
True shepherds lead the flock
To pastures fresh and large.
Where waters flow from Rock.

Be watchful night and day,
Of grievous wolves beware.
They aim to draw away
Those lambs for whom you care.
With lowliness of mind,
And e'en perchance a tear,
Press on, look not behind
Or count your life too dear.

If, with great urgency,
You go with "spirit bound",
With bonds abiding thee,
Unmoved may you be found.
Then, shun not to declare
The Gospel of God's Grace,
As if your hearers were
No more to see your face.

What glory in "that day",
The day of grand review,
To hear Chief Shepherd say
"There is a crown for you!
Your work was tending sheep.
You fed them, kept them near,
Oft losing rest and sleep,
Your rest is *with Me here*".

* * * * *

10: Regular Service

Our involvement in the Lord's work in Harman's Cross dates from the time we married in 1931, when a weekly meeting for young people was conducted in our house. We both had been engaged in this work for several years, Joan conducting her class along C.S.S.M. (Children's Special Service Mission) lines in her home in Swanage, and I in the Gospel Hall at Herston. This new meeting continued in our house until the early days of the war, when a wooden building that was no longer required by an evangelist was handed over for our use. It was erected on a plot next to the bungalow and services were held every Sunday, and also a school in the afternoons.

The Lord prospered this, and a number found the Saviour in that little hut. With sometimes as many as forty people listening attentively, they were days to be remembered by many. One old man, who at one time could have profited by Mother's mouth wash, came regularly and often asked for the hymn "We love Thy House, O Lord". I found great encouragement when he told me he was trusting the Lord Jesus. Some weeks after I had taken him to a Rest Home I met him in the street, a different man altogether. His first words were, "When you put me down that day, they put me into a bath. I thought it was going to finish me, but I felt better for it!" Clean inside and outside, was my silent reflection! Visiting him some months later in hospital, just before he died, he said, "I'm soon going up along wi' Mum!" This was his wife; and it was another case of prayers for loved ones being answered years later.

I remember once giving an opportunity for someone to give a testimony, hoping that a young man sitting at the rear would break the ice. Instead, to my surprise, an elderly lady rose and came to the front to tell us how she was brought to the Lord. We later found her to be the widow of a one-time Lord Mayor of London. Her name was Lady Studd, and she was visiting her lifelong friend, Princess Trobetzkoy, who was also present on that occasion. Well might we sing, "What a gathering of the ransomed that will be!"

I am amazed at the miscellany of speakers who have helped me over the years, men from all walks of life. Not all from the same church background, but their message was the same, its basis being "Jesus Christ and Him crucified": a message of hope with assurance. One such man was Arthur Gook, a missionary who during the war was acting Consul in Iceland. He wrote a book, "Can a Young Man Trust His Bible?", which helped me a great deal.

The pulpit in that Mission hut, which is still being used in the chapel known as Woodside, came from the little school at Bushey, near Corfe Castle, which belonged to the Church and served both education and worship. The helpful thing about this pulpit is that the speaker is enclosed by it, so that there will be no walking about: he remains behind the Book!

Running a motor business that was growing in size, and being responsible for the Lord's work at Harman's Cross, together with eldership in the Gospel Hall at Swanage, will shed some light on the hardships my wife and family were faced with over a number of years. I was to learn again that I needed the Lord's control in my own life, a subject I had been preaching to others for years!

If I am asked about my prayer life at the time, "Difficult" would be the short answer, but I want to enlarge on that. Bringing members of my family into focus, as I have done, bears witness that God is all that He claims to be to us, in spite of what we are!

A book that has helped is "Prayer", by O. Hallesby (it is still in print). In it he insists that prayer and helplessness are inseparable. The apostle Paul discovered this and found the answer. He writes: "I can do all things through Christ who strengthens me" (Philippians 4:13).

To keep my mind from drifting while in prayer was often a problem. For some years I have found help in praying aloud, but only when aware it was out of reach of human ears. When walking my dog in the lanes Shep would sometimes think it was he that was being addressed! I have been encouraged to find others who pray aloud whenever opportunity allows. With one such I had an unexpected encounter.

Sitting in my car with Shep perched beside me, both very satisfied with our walk and about to drive away, I heard running footsteps from behind. This stranger informed me that he was following his doctor's instructions relating to an insomnia problem, but was now facing another problem through exhaustion with two miles to go where his wife awaited him! Once he was comfortably settled into the back seat of my car, it was not long before I discovered I was talking to Canon J. B. Phillips, whose translation of the New Testament I often found so helpful. It was when the conversation centred on how in wakefulness to occupy the hours of darkness, and I suggested praying audibly, that he told me he was doing just that in the lane before he spotted my car!

When praying audibly, the tone of voice reveals the measure of earnestness in much the same way as when people speak to us. I am glad, though, that the Lord hears the inaudible too, even bending his ear to hear what I say. How patient He is! "Because he has inclined his ear unto me, therefore will I call upon him as long as I live" (Psalm 116:2).

The Christian life is a battle, and in ceasing to pray we cease to fight. Too often we fail to give it the priority demanded and somehow kid ourselves that something else is more important. I hope my reader is still with me, because the hand of the Lord will be seen as He deals in His love with my problem.

For my various responsibilities were becoming a burden as I allowed my activity-orientated life to encroach

Regular Service

upon time which I knew would have been better spent — indeed, needed to be spent — in waiting upon the Lord to seek that He have His own way in every department of my busy life. The result was not only a nagging feeling of guilt, accompanied by an awareness that I was failing to cope adequately with what I was doing, but the onset of a nervous disability which put me out of useful service for several years, both in church and in business; the latter would have folded had it not been for a loyal staff who realised my plight.

Before getting so low, I loved speaking to travellers and others about my faith, but now I was avoiding all personal contacts by leaving via the back door, thankful for the trees behind! I recall taking this step when a high-powered rep. called — the very last person I wanted to see! The shade under the nut trees, and the birds doing their bit, were bliss indeed, until my eye drifted towards a gap only a few yards away. There, to my horror, was this man, crouched down, watching me! I pretended I did not see him, and from that he got the message. For me, it was no laughing matter, just one of relief when he went. Even to sit through a service sometimes was sheer agony, and, on occasions, unendurable.

When my doctor was asked how long I would have to rely on the medication, his reply was, "As long as necessary." I knew that was what the Lord was saying to me about my manner of life and His corrective measures. This troubled me because the truth was getting through that my biggest problem was not physical, but spiritual. The two are more closely allied than we imagine, and if we don't attend to it the Lord will, because He loves us.

I was aware that David once said, "Let me fall now into the hand of the LORD; for very great are his mercies" (1 Chronicles 21:13). So, casting myself on Him, I put the tablets in the drawer and found myself no worse without them. After a month I realised I was talking to people I had avoided.

Since that time, there have been occasions when the Lord has needed to remind me that nothing but blessing can follow when we, as believers, allow Him to deal with us as He sees fit.

Pain and suffering are mysteries to us, as God intended them to be, but He gives us enough light in His Word to trust Him, and the Scriptures are clear that not all suffering is the result of some particular transgression. The object in view might well be that His children should better know His loving heart (see, for example, John 9:1-3). I will enlarge on this subject before expressing my thoughts on 'healing'.

A well-known surgeon, surrounded by some young people, was asked in my hearing about his job, and, "did he enjoy carving people up?", to which he replied, "I love it!". But when asked his position when ill, his prompt reply was that he first asked the Lord what lesson He wanted him to learn, and followed it with a request for help to learn it quickly!

Pain is a problem often discussed among Christians, and some have passed through times that leave my nervous trouble a mere nuisance! I am thinking of two men in particular. God had been able to trust both with an experience that would prove to be a blessing in their work for Him, and this is how one put it to me: "I didn't know that God sometimes allows His children to pass through such a degree of pain; it was incessant for days on end. I didn't want to read or pray, or even listen to others doing it for me! I felt abandoned. Then, in His mercy, God saw fit to act and, Oh!, what a relief, what a joy, to find Him still there, where He had been all the time!"

This was not an isolated case. More recently, a friend who for years had been engaged in hospital visitation, and had passed through the same experience, told me he was longing to get back to the wards. "But", he said, "it will not be the same man!" He had learned a lot about himself, and about his Lord, to Whom he was now looking for help in speaking a word suitable for the suffering.

I once accompanied a friend of school days on a weekend visit to our old home town, so full of memories, good and otherwise. Whilst there, we paid what we thought would be a 'pastoral' visit to an old lady who had been confined to bed since a young woman; my friend knew her but, although Mother visited her often, I never saw her. She could do nothing for herself; in fact, she told us there were times when she would pray that the wasp flying about the room would not settle on her nose! Neighbours on both sides seemed able and willing to meet her needs and no doubt were on the receiving end spiritually, as we were that day. This woman was radiant with the joy of the Lord whom she had known since a child. Knowing the reason for our visit, she made sure we would not be leaving without a word of encouragement ourselves!

I have often been asked if I believe in divine healing, and I certainly do, but I have reservations about its place in the church today, having, for some years, taken the view that certain gifts of the Spirit — such as speaking in tongues, prophecy, healing — ceased as signs (which they were) with the apostles. It would appear that history confirms this. I found that this view was held by the man I visited in Poole and who told me he had spoken in tongues on many occasions.

There are two scriptures which have a bearing on sickness due to transgression. I have referred to one passage in which Paul calls for self-examination (1 Corinthians 11:31-32). But James says: "Is any sick among you? Let him call for the elders of the church; and let them pray over him, anointing him with oil in the name of the Lord: and the prayer of faith shall save the sick, and the Lord shall raise him up; and if he has committed sins, they shall be forgiven him" (James 5:14-15).

If I were called upon to do this service, I would be very unhappy in rejecting the call, because that passage in James is, to me, very clear.

I have referred to memories that were revived with a visit to Shaftesbury, and if my reader is waiting for something of an "otherwise" quality (mentioned above), I shall disappoint him! But I can say my friend and I had much pleasure in re-living pushing each other into the dark, rat-infested corn bins of Stratton Sons and Mead (where his father worked), where rats, imaginary or real, joined us; also drinking marble-bottled lemonade made in the same building in Barton Hill; bathing in the town swimming pool; winter skating on Wincombe Pond; and, of course, Ebenezer Gospel Hall, of which only the site now remained. In short, it was Shaftesbury, the "city set on a hill", where we both came into a personal relationship with our Saviour Jesus Christ. But I must return to my subject.

The story is well-worn, but still has a message, of the carriage spring maker. Speaking to a friend as he worked the bellows for another heat-up before plunging the red-hot metal into the water, he said, "Sometimes I say to the Lord, 'Put me into the fire and into the water, but, please Lord, don't put me on the scrap-heap!' " This man knew his Bible and his Lord and, without doubt, himself also!

I reject the view that sinless perfection is possible this side of heaven, and Romans 7 seems to indicate that it was not Paul's view; two parts of him are having a real tug-of-war! These are the law of God, in which he delights, and the law of sin, which was in his body. He says: "O wretched man that I am! Who shall deliver me ...?" (Romans 7:24).

Of course, if Paul had left it there, he would have had no message for us; but in chapter 8 he has discovered another law. He calls it "the law of the Spirit of life in Jesus Christ" (v.2), and this law was going to do what the first law, given on Mount Sinai, could never do, though

Regular Service

he delighted in it. The Ten Commandments are very good, because they reveal the character of God, but they have no power to save anyone, only condemn them — as the Colonel I have referred to discovered when dying. From now on, Paul is no longer struggling to be good, he is allowing the indwelling Holy Spirit to have His way, and, as he does this, victory is assured. He says: "... in all these things we are more than conquerors through Him that loved us" (Romans 8:37).

The man who helped me in the office — and gave me the dig concerning my aversion to paying income tax! — told me to read blocks of Scripture at a time; for example, Romans 5 and 6, then 7 and 8; and it is amazing how the verses explain each other. The Bible becomes alive as its truth unfolds.

It is clear that Paul accepted the Genesis account of creation as history; Adam as real a person as Jesus. The first brought us sin and death; the Second, life and peace. For Paul, it all fitted into place in his thinking on the road to Damascus — light from heaven, in every sense of the word!

It was once put to me this way: "God sees only two men: Adam and Christ. The first brought sin and death, the Second, life and peace. Under which headship do you come?

Mention should be made of Gwyneth Rogers, whose help as receptionist and secretary I appreciated greatly after the war; her husband, Captain Rogers, also looked after the accounts. Being a great-granddaughter of the explorer David Livingstone, the biography of whom was familiar to us both, the conversation drifted at times to things that motivated that outstanding man who, under God's guiding hand, laid down his life for the Africa of today.

[The narrative continues in Chapter 12, on page 132]

11: Hymns

In the decade following the Second World War the pressures of business life were making their mark on spirit, soul and body. Yet it was then that time was given to the composition of hymns — music as well as words.

My efforts to improve on a well known Sankey tune for one of the hymns below drew from a kind friend the remark that he viewed it as an "improvement in reverse"! I am therefore not disappointed that in these pages only the words appear!

Though from time to time I have questioned the value of these efforts, I fall back on the premise that if the hand of God was in the writing, then it can if He wills also be in the reading, and it is in this spirit that what follows is presented.

* * * * *

CAESAREA PHILIPPI

I have found the greatest treasure
One can ever find today.
Its true value who can measure?
To possess it who can pay?
Men by searching find it never. —
For they know not where it lies. —
Yet it can be theirs, and ever
Change the outlook of their lives.

I found Christ by revelation;
God revealed His Son to me.
I rejoice in His salvation;
Things are different, I am free.
How the enemy distorted
Every truth about my Lord!
Satan's evil purpose thwarted,
Christ is now by me adored.

I now find God has a purpose
For my life, He has design.

It is now a thing most precious
And in fact no longer mine.
He has bought me, I'm His treasure!
Why? I cannot understand,
But I know God looks for pleasure
In the product of His hand.

Jesus tells me that to follow
Must be now my chief concern.
At His feet, beneath His shadow,
Is the place where I can learn,
"Set my sight, Lord, clear my vision,
Show me, Lord, Thy love for men;
Help me heed Thy Great Commission,
Cleanse me, send me unto them."

* * * * *

I LOVE THE LORD
(based on Psalm 116)

I love the Lord because He heard my voice.
He loosed my bonds, and makes my heart rejoice,
Inclines His ear to things I have to say;
That's why I call upon the Lord each day.

Trouble was near, and I was very low.
Empty my life, and often tears would flow.
It was just there I called upon His Name,
And from that day things have not been the same.

Before my Lord I now desire to walk,
About my Lord I find I wish to talk.
Unto my Lord my vows I now will pay,
For in my Lord I find my joy today.

Then come with me, if you are of like mind,
Into His courts, for there it is we find
His people meet, His Name to praise and bless.
Praise ye the Lord, He is our righteousness!

* * * * *

THE NEW BIRTH

"As many as received Him
To them gave He the power
To be the sons of God" —
The very sons of God!
For they who on His Name believe,
And in their hearts the Christ receive,
"Become the sons of God".

As many as reject Him
Do not possess this right;
The privilege of sonship
Is not for sons of night.
To them God must remain unknown —
His loving Fatherhood alone
Belongs to "sons of God".

The wise will then receive Him
And get things settled now.
With joy He will receive them
When at His feet they bow.
Then saved alone by sovereign grace
He freely gives them each a place
Among the "sons of God".

He soon will bring to glory
These erstwhile sons of night!
A great, amazing story
Of grace equating might.
Their song has now sweet melody,
A theme for all eternity
For "many sons" of God.

* * * * *

THE NEW LOOK

God is Light, God is Love, Christ came down from above
   To a world of lost sinners he came.
By His grace I now see that His love was for me.
   By His death I have life through His Name
O! what can I do as one now born anew
   That will show that I love Him indeed?
His will would I know, then obedience will show
   That I love Him Who met all my need.

Ever true to His Name He is ever the same.
   But in me can men see aught of Him?
Do they see in my walk, do they note by my talk
   That His joy fills my heart to the brim?
Am I walking in love with His strength from above?
   For 'tis living the life that will tell.
If with unveilèd face I'm reflecting His grace,
   They will long to know Jesus as well.

I must walk in the Light, doing that which is right,
   Ever seeking His will to obey.
Then my heart will rejoice at the sound of His voice
   As to me He doth speak by the way.
Oh! what can I give unto Him while I live,
   Unto Him Who is made Lord of all?
If for Him set apart, He must have all my heart,
   Then for service I'll wait for His call.

* * * * *

AT HOME

Lord, may our home on which we seek Thy blessing
Be marked with joy, a-blending praise with prayer.
With such control in times of ease or testing
It will be noised abroad that Christ is there.

Even the music and the conversation,
Ripples of laughter, things that make it "home" —
When Christ is there, amazing revelation!
His joy and pleasure is amongst His own.

If each new day begins with careful reading
From that one Book, so true, so up-to-date,
It will be seen that God Himself is leading,
And nothing happens there by chance or fate.

'Twil be observed the door is always open,
And welcome given to sad and aching hearts.
His love compels, and this is but the token:
All needed strength His gracious hand imparts.

If skies are grey, and things become depressing —
Intruding clouds have somewhat hid His face —
Whisper His Name, and, all your need confessing,
Soon you will hear, "Sufficient is My grace".

It is His lips that speak of heavenly mansions,
Meanwhile 'tis clear His will for us is this.
Letting Him rule, rejoicing in His sanctions,
Our homes can be a foretaste of that bliss.

* * * * *

MY SHEPHERD

The Good Shepherd loves His sheep,
Guarding them while they sleep.
On waking, still the same,
Calling them each by name.
Sometimes they disobey.
But there's no other way,
And never will they find
A Guide so true and kind.

The Good Shepherd leads His sheep.
Close to His feet they keep.
Grand hills on which they roam,
Safe Guide to see them Home.
And yet they sometimes stray,
Seeking some other way.
Good Shepherd knows where best
Those paths that lead to rest.

The Good Shepherd seeks His sheep,
Oft crossing valleys deep.
Bears on His shoulders strong
Those who to Him belong.
Passing through sorrow's flood
He bought them with His blood.
No one can touch His lambs
Or snatch them from His hands.

The Good Shepherd comforts sheep
When age forbids them leap.
Gently He leads them on
To heights where He is gone.
Skies that are overcast
Shall break with light at last.
Folded within yon' Door
Are joys for evermore.

* * * * *

NEW THINGS

If any man be in Christ,
If any man be in Christ,
He is a new creation,
Made whole through God's salvation.
Old things have passed away,
For night has turned to day.
Behold! ... Behold!
All things are made new.

His mind is now renewed,
And with new powers endued
New songs he now is singing,
And praise to God is bringing.
In Christ he is complete;
His place is at His feet.
He there ... through prayer
Puts on the new man.

All things are now of God.
All things are now of God,
Who reconciled him to Him
Through Jesus Christ the Lord.
No eye as yet has seen,
No ear has ever heard,
What God ... hath prepared
For them that love Him.

When heaven and earth are new,
And former things are through —
No sea, no sin, no sorrow,
No yesterday or morrow,
No tears and no more pain —
New things will new remain.
Behold! ... I come!
Amen, Lord, so come.

* * * * *

THE EASY YOKE

What has no excess elation,
Nor unduly is cast down,
Never touched by ostentation,
Though it always wears a crown?
'Tis the meek and quiet spirit
That possesses untold wealth,
Unassertive ever is it,
Quite unoccupied with self.

It is likened to apparel,
To a garment that is fair,
Seeking not the world's approval
Or its graces fondly air.
But it has the approbation
Of the Lord, who is its source.
It is that self-abnegation
That will never know remorse.

They are God's victorious people
That display this lovely flower.
Far from being weak and feeble,
They possess a hidden power.
With its soothing fragrant action,
Meekness works like healing balm.
By dispelling cause of faction,
Stormy seas become a calm.

Oh! that we could see more clearly
Jesu's meek and lowly heart!
Many things we hold so dearly
We would gladly bid depart.
This no dreary imposition,
Think on what may be our own!
For this grace, this disposition,
Has its hand upon God's throne.

* * * * *

TRANSCENDENCY

Our Lord has transcendent glory,
Surpassing man's highest thought.
Though worlds are on Him dependent
Yet by many unknown, unsought.
Eternal, as Son with the Father.
In time He incarnate became.
Through death it was His to gather
A people to praise His Name.

Perfection in fullest measure,
God's will was His true delight.
The centre of all God's pleasure,
No deflection to left or right.
His life is our perfect example,
His death has secured our release.
With heaven we gaze and marvel
At Him who is now "our Peace".

Consider His omnipresence,
He filleth all time and space.
No less than true God in essence
That has entered the human race!
Omnipotent, also all-knowing,
Unchanging, life-giver is He.
With love and compassion glowing
His heart moves in sympathy.

Infallible as the Teacher,
Unique in simplicity.
To honest and thoughtful seeker
All His words have finality.
That equal with God He gives token
By sending His Spirit to men.
His promises ne'er are broken,
He soon will appear again.

* * * * *

WHY THE CROSS?

How cold the world when Jesus came,
So few believed on His dear Name.
To such He gave and giveth still
The right of sons; this is God's will.
They share His life, born from above.
They know His voice, and Him they love.
His perfect love has stilled their fears,
And warmed their heart and dried their tears.

How wonderful! But why the Cross?
And why such shame and utter loss?
The wonder is, that working then
We see God's hand, and those of men.
The rebel man would treat Him so:
To all His claims he answers "No!"
But God Himself must turn away
From Christ, the sinless One that day.

Three hours of darkness shrouds the hill —
Withal a place of gloom — until
A sudden cry! by many heard,
And from the Cross there comes this word:
"Finished it is!" The work is done,
And sinners now to God may run!
For access has been freely made,
And they who come are not afraid.

The chains of sin for them are loosed.
To God they have been introduced!
Approach is made, and that by One
Who is none less than God's own Son.
The awful Cross was not for nought.
His risen life to men has brought
Glad joy and rest, and God's own peace
That does with passing days increase.

* * * * *

12: Under Instruction

I come now to the sequel in my story, as it relates to Father's closing days. Unlike a man I knew, he didn't find deafness a 'comfortable affliction' (neither does his son!), nor was he pleased when I had difficulty in obtaining parts for his car! Then, quite suddenly, he realised his days for having the last word were over, and, in accepting this, he became happier. So much so that for the next two years I found it no hardship that my movements were clearly defined, now that he would feed out of my hand! With some outside help, it was a privilege to attend to his needs, because we were closer than ever before. Both at home and in the hospital, his last days were marked by expressions of gratitude.

I have referred to his grasp of the Scriptures, and particularly the teaching in Romans on the security of the believer. One incident in this connection I will never forget. I went to his room to find him in tears.

"It's my sins", he said.

He was talking to the right person on that subject, because it gave me joy to remind him of what God had done with our sins.

"I know that! I know that!" he shouted, wanting the last word again, "but I'm sorry that I grieved the Lord!"

I had come into his room while he was contemplating the cost of his forgiveness, as I do when I come to the Lord's Table. Like Peter by the lake, he had been telling the Lord that he loved Him. The two letters written by the man who denied his Lord reveal the marvel of God's grace. We are encouraged to press on trustingly to the finishing post and he tells us how it is done. Peter never forgot that moment when, in the Upper Room, and after some protest, he allowed the Lord to wash his feet!

Father had been a help to many along the lines of his own experience, but how sad that his elder brother, whose ministry had been so blessed of God, was unable to finish the race with the same note of triumph that came from Father's lips as he lay in hospital. He had no need to exaggerate now in order to make his point: "I've got the Everlasting Arms underneath!", he said.

I have said earlier that we are safe, and only safe, when we keep close to the Lord, and for this we need the support of fellow believers. I feel this to be the thrust of the Lord's teaching on washing one another's feet (John 13).

We anticipate with joy seeing our loved ones again, and I look forward to meeting these two brothers and, through grace, adding my quota to their song:

> *Let us with joy adopt the strain*
> *We hope to sing for ever there —*
> *Worthy the Lamb for sinners slain,*
> *Worthy alone the crown to wear.*
>
> *Without one thought that's good to plead,*
> *Oh, what could shield us from despair*
> *But this, though we are vile indeed*
> *The Lord our Righteousness is there?*
>
> (Samuel Rutherford)

A man of the same name once said he was a complexity of three very different persons: the first being the one that is known to his fellows; the second known only to himself, and very different! — but it is the third John who is the real John, and he is known by God alone.

Whilst speaking at a service held in the local hospital, I found myself suddenly joined in talk by an elderly patient lying in a bed close to me, and surrounded by her relatives. In her joy at seeing me (I don't think I was mistaken!), and in a voice far above mine for the ward to hear, she said, "I know that man, I do, ever since he was young. I could tell you quite a lot about him, I could!" Being unable to compete, the prepared message was abandoned and that of the 'three Johns' given instead — what I am in the eyes of others, in my own eyes, and in

God's eyes — seeking to make it clear that the need of all three could be met by the Lord Jesus.

My 'ego' always got a boost when someone said nice things about me or the business; but if other people were listening I would go all on edge, fearing a voice would pipe up with, "But listen to me! . . ."

The Lord had a word for His disciples facing the same enemy. In Luke 6:26 we read: "Woe unto you, when all men shall speak well of you . . . "; while, at the close of the Old Testament, the Lord says through Malachi: "Therefore take heed to your spirit . . . " (Malachi 2:15).

During the war, I was having my hair cut by a woman who was standing in for my usual hairdresser, and as the job was in progress she enquired where I lived. On learning that Harman's Cross was the district, the next question, put in a rather enigmatical tone of voice, was, "Anywhere near that Foley?" The quick change in the conversation which resulted from my reply that I was "that Foley" left me somewhat bewildered and, I am sure, prompted some needed heart-searching — although I only went in for a hair cut!

Taking this thought a little further, the apostle Paul ends his letter to the Galatians with these words: "I bear in my body the marks of the Lord Jesus", and then follows it up with: "The *grace* of our Lord Jesus Christ be with your spirit" (Galatians 6:17-18).

A recent speaker at Woodside Chapel was the boy who had been involved with the bicycle that collapsed, Harold Foster. Chatting with him at the close of the service, this subject was enlarged on with reference to his father, a man who, in my view, radiated Christ.

"Dad", he said, "sought to live like Paul — with a conscience void of offence toward God and man."

Still speaking of his father, the conversation found balance in recalling the occasion of his angry outburst: "I would like to give both you boys a good thrashing!" We had, through our own inattentiveness, caused him inconvenience and embarrassment by giving him the wrong time of train arrival when he was going to collect his daughter from the station. I am sure that I, simply by being present at the time, saved my friend from being 'seat-warmed' that day! No doubt he will concur with this quotation, again from Malachi: "My covenant was with him of life and peace; and I gave them to him for the fear wherewith he feared me, and was afraid before my name. The law of truth was in his mouth, and iniquity was not found in his lips: he walked with me in peace and equity, and did turn many away from iniquity" (Malachi 2:5-6).

Both Harold and I have cause to thank God for parents who instructed us concerning not only the love of God, but also his authority.

* * * * *

FRUIT OF THE SPIRIT

I want to know more of God's grace in my soul,
Long-suff'ring and meekness with calm self-control.
More faith, love, and patience, more kindness and joy —
These peaceable fruits that no power can destroy.

The works of the flesh bring their problems untold,
And profit us nothing, as time will unfold.
To walk in the Spirit means God has His way,
And victory's assured, with His strength for each day.

'Tis said that the path of a Christian is tame!
Yet many have laid down their lives for His Name.
How thrilling the joys will that pathway provide
When Jesus is there very close to our side.

Have we lost our joy? Has the vision grown dim?
Then back to those paths that are pleasing to Him.
Oh, fill me, Lord Jesus, I long that You'll see
The Spirit's own fruit, there abounding in me.

* * * * *

A SUNDIAL IN ANGEL SQUARE

During his ministry, our Lord was often questioned by people steeped in tradition, and those who taught these 'man-made counterfeits' received His strongest condemnation. Their followers are with us today, and in most cases are quite satisfied. Religious, but with little knowledge of the Bible and its message of redemption, they are resting on a false security.

When speaking to an officer in the Tank Corps, a quiet, thoughtful man with whom I had had several conversations previously, I asked if I could spend an hour at his home with an open Bible. "No," he said, "I'm not prepared to call into question the teaching of my church!" It was clear that his church and its ministers were the final authority for his faith, but just where he stood in his relationship with the Lord Jesus I was never sure.

I was giving a driving lesson to a lady whose husband no longer drove and she was mastering the art well; so well, perhaps, there was a tendency for the conversation to drift on to this all-important topic, in the course of which I quoted the verse that led to my father's conversion. It runs: "He that hears my word, and believes on him that sent me, has everlasting life, and shall not come into condemnation; but is passed from death unto life" (John 5:24).

"Where did you get that?" she asked.

When I told her that these were the words of the Lord Jesus, she asked me to repeat them, which I did. I had reason to believe the subject was talked over with her husband, who took the same view as the officer. It was not raised again.

Still on the subject of traditions, a retired Brigadier General who had served in India — Frost by name, whom I knew well, he having preached on several occasions in the Gospel Hall at Swanage — had a similar background to the two already mentioned, and had been held captive by what he called a "spurious Christianity". He was so incensed at being caught by the erroneous teaching that he pulled no punches in dealing with those who propagated it! Nevertheless, the Lord blessed his ministry as an evangelist. With the early teaching I received, I have no need to take this strong line, but a minister did once tell me that we evangelicals can be very unkind towards them sometimes. "Many of our men are in the dark and need help, and if you want to get their ear a softer line of approach is needed", was how he put it.

My wife recently received a distressing letter from an old acquaintance who had just lost her husband. The priest had told her that he could offer no hope for her dear husband, because he had not attended Mass. Realising she needed comfort, we made the long journey and were able to speak of One who said, "I know their sorrows", and Who is indeed the "God of all comfort", and not unmindful of hers.

She listened very attentively as we spoke of the Lord Jesus, but it is the Spirit of God alone who can open the eyes of those that are blinded by the "father of lies". Both the Bible and history show that Satan leads men to lust after power and distorts truth in order to do so. All error contains an element of truth to make it acceptable.

My deep longing to lead a person to Christ has a danger, and it lies in myself. Far too often have I placed, perhaps unconsciously, undue confidence in the power of argument when seeking to help people to faith in Christ, in cases winning the argument but losing the man.

The power of the Holy Spirit is held back when we get in His way, and I recall one occasion when I smarted (and profited!) under His gentle chiding. I was manning the pumps one evening when a customer pulled in, ostensibly for petrol, but in reality to continue a broken conversation begun the same morning concerning God's way of salvation.

As we talked I felt things were going well, until an old friend, who didn't expect the garage to be open, braked hard and pulled in for a fill-up. Raymond Scott-Mitchell was hurrying back to London but, as he handed me the cash in the presence of this other customer, I put to him the question that we had just been discussing, and then left the two men talking as I locked up the pumps.

It was then that I overheard something I was sure the Lord wanted me to hear. It went something like this: "Thank you. Mr Foley didn't put it over to me like that. You have helped a lot." They parted with a warmth that spoke volumes. My friend continued his journey, no doubt thanking the Lord for the opportunity given; the writer, to his house deep in thought!

This sort of thing must have happened on a number of occasions. Sometimes lessons have to be repeated — and the Lord is able to overrule my blunders, as He did on that occasion.

Quite recently, a lady told me that she hadn't liked the little talk that took place some years before, but she added, "I am glad you spoke as you did, for it was my awakening."

(Since writing this, she has been called to be with the Lord, suddenly, in a road accident.)

In following the example of the Lord Jesus, in no way should we ever be aggressive, but as Christians we have a responsibility to warn of the danger in neglecting God's way of life (for the unexpected often happens). If people are blind to their being on the wrong road, it should not be offensive to inform them that God has said: "All have sinned, and come short . . . " (Romans 3:23). To sinners who repent, the gospel is very good news. We read: "The Father sent the Son to be the Saviour of the world" (1 John 4:14). The Son says: "I am the way, the truth, and the life: no man comes to the Father, but by me" (John 14:6).

The sin question has now become the Son question. Pilate realised this when he said, "What shall I do with Jesus?" and then foolishly answered it by washing his hands!

Many years later, the apostle John commented on this

Under Instruction

with these words: "He came unto His own, and His own received Him not. But as many as received Him, to them gave He power to become the sons of God, even to them that believe on His name" (John 1:11-12).

I am glad that I belong to that family, all by the mercy of God.

It is the common experience of Christians to find the Lord overruling the mistakes of His children, and, particularly for those young in the faith, this gives encouragement. I had invited a man who had recently come to the Lord to join me in a meeting at Wareham, all with the view to helping him in his new life. I was also looking forward to hearing the speaker, Mr Jack Field, whom I knew well and thought would be very suitable for the occasion.

As my friend took his seat in the car I sensed something was wrong, and the cause I was soon to be told. Apparently, he and the gardener had just had a disagreement that ended in verbal abuse, reminiscent of pre-conversion days.

"I thought I had finished with all that, Jack! Do Christians ever lose their temper?"

After giving him the short answer I sought to enlarge, and in doing so we were late in arriving; but it so happened that our speaker was also late, having been held up on the road. With a brief introduction, we hurried into the chapel to find the meeting had started, but with Donald Scott, whom I also knew, at the desk. It was clear that someone had made a mistake in the booking, and so I was not in a very happy frame of mind! But as the service proceeded it became very clear that the hand of the Lord was on at least two of us, and maybe on the other latecomer! The reading was taken from Psalm 37, and the verses that were enlarged on were 23 and 24. They read: "The steps of a good man are ordered by the Lord: and he delights in his way. Though he fall, he shall not be utterly cast down: for the Lord upholds him with his hand."

The psalm is so true of the man who is seeking to walk in God's ways. And, as he does so, David is encouraging him to place his full confidence in God to keep him safe from an enemy who is bent on destroying his faith. The issue is in God's hands: "... he shall not be utterly cast down ... ".

As I, a mature believer as opposed to one who was a mere 'babe in Christ', listened that evening, I could not but reflect that those occasions when Satan caught me on the wrong foot could have been avoided, if more care had been given to my prayer life. My friend was very excited on the way home, not only because of help received, but especially the circumstances in which it came. I don't recall the sequel to the problem with the gardener, if I ever knew, but if the message found its mark he would have found it a privilege to witness for his Lord by way of an apology, and real joy would have followed.

It is interesting to note that, in His Sermon on the Mount, the Lord quotes verse 11 of that psalm: "Blessed are the meek: for they shall inherit the earth" (Matthew 5:5). Meekness is not weakness. It was the strongest of men who said these words before His crucifixion, and, as I write, they still hold good: "Come unto me, all ye that labour and are heavy laden, and I will give you rest. Take my yoke upon you, and learn of me; for I am meek and lowly in heart: and ye shall find rest unto your souls. For my yoke is easy, and my burden is light" (Matthew 11:28-30).

This leads me back to reflect upon my own progress since my Christian baptism, and it will be seen that since that happy, yet solemn, occasion at the age of fifteen there has been some growth, though the progress may have been slow and certainly often painful; I still have a long way to go, and with little time left.

This natural heart is still "prone to wander, prone to leave the God I love". So, I read in Leviticus 20:24-26, "I am the Lord your God, which have separated you from other people ... and ye shall be holy unto me: for I the

Lord am holy, and have severed you from the other people, that ye should be mine."

I like to link these words with those of the Lord Jesus: "My sheep hear my voice, and I know them, and they follow me" (John 10:27).

If those Jews to whom He was speaking repented and believed on Him, they would have found themselves under a new directive — a change of masters, One who says, "If you love me, you will keep my words."

Baptism is associated with following Jesus, and just prior to His return to heaven He told His disciples to go into all the world and preach the gospel, ". . . baptising them into the Name of the Father, and of the Son, and of the Holy Spirit" (Matthew 28:19).

Days later, in Jerusalem, thousands heard Peter and the apostles preach the message of a crucified and risen Christ. They believed it and were baptised.

The person submitting to this ordinance is *publicly* acknowledging in effect, "My sins deserve death, but Jesus the Son of God has taken my place, so I take this step in acknowledgment that I belong to Him, and from now on I will seek to live the new life that began when He saved me."

Baptism in water speaks very vividly of death, burial and resurrection, but other figures are used in Scripture concerning this ordinance. Paul speaks of it as the taking off of an old garment and the putting on of a new (Colossians 3:9-10). The old is buried, the new emerges. From now on we are to reckon ourselves dead unto sin, but alive to God (Romans 6:11). To "reckon" is to thoughtfully consider — to keep in front of me, that I have done with the wretched thing that caused my Lord His death.

This constant reckoning is essential if we are going to experience victory over sin day by day, and if I had paid more heed to that injunction much sadness caused by selfishness and pride would have been avoided.

Someone may ask, "Shall I be able to keep it up, if I am baptised?" The answer will be "No" if we do not continue to do this reckoning day by day, constantly coming back to our Lord for cleansing, and seeking His strength to live the new life.

I know of no scripture that would support the practice of infant sprinkling, and observation leads me to believe that many people rely on the action and promises of their parents for their security, knowing nothing of their need to be "born again" (John 3:3 — the words of Jesus).

It should be noted that nearly all the references in the book of the Acts speak of baptism following believing: it is an act of the will. Jesus, the sinless Son of God, submitted to the baptism of John, this being the sign of His commitment to His Father's will; and, if we love Him, we too will want to take this humbling step in glad token of our obedience.

At the time of writing, this subject has been much on my mind, having had the joy of baptising a man of my own age who has recently come to the Lord. We had done much business with him over the years, but I do not recall ever speaking with him on spiritual matters. God had spoken to him through the sickness and death of a daughter. Well advanced as a physicist, Ken Collins is now taking his place as a child in God's school. "Let's have it simple, Jack, or I can't take it" was how he put it to express his hunger. There are no short cuts, we all have to come that way.

This ordinance is followed by that of Communion, or the Lord's Supper. I have been using the term 'Lord's Table', because it was instituted by Him on the night of His betrayal. These were His words as He broke the bread on that occasion: "Do this in remembrance of me". Those who love Him want to do this as often as they are able, but always with hearts prepared. The apostle Paul enlarges on this in his first letter to the Christians in Corinth (1 Corinthians 11:23-32).

Under Instruction

In recalling childhood days earlier in my narrative, I described this worship meeting when believers met to remember the Lord in the manner carried out by those of Paul's day, and after. Seventy years have passed since I watched Mother, with others like-minded, partake of the bread and wine. They didn't come to listen to a sermon, or the preaching of the gospel — there were other occasions for these. They came to worship the Lord in the way that He appointed. The hymns, readings of Scriptures, and prayers all centred on the person and work of the Lord Jesus, and they would allow nothing to hinder them from bringing their tribute of thanksgiving.

If the Holy Spirit is unhindered as different brothers lead the worship, a spontaneity of thought and freedom of expression are very marked. Strangers attending are often amazed that nothing has been pre-arranged. For many, including the writer, the Sunday worship meeting is the acme of the week, and the Lord still invites me to sit at His Table as occasion permits. Very often, before leaving, I recall words spoken to the (now cleansed) demon-possessed man: "Go home to thy friends, and tell them how great things the Lord hath done for thee ... " (Mark 5:19).

In the early days of the Church, Christians carried out this ordinance on Sunday, the day following the Jewish sabbath, a practice that to a great extent holds today; this being the day that Jesus rose from the dead.

Sabbath-keeping stands out in its importance all through the Old Testament. For man, it was to be a day of rest, dating back to creation, and was God's rest until broken by man's disobedience. Thereafter, it was viewed by God as a test of man's obedience to His will, placing it fourth in the Commandments. Israel's history in this respect is a sad story, and is enlarged on by Ezekiel in chapter 20, where God speaks of "My sabbaths" (verses 11-12). Christians have carried this thought on to Sunday, by calling it the "Lord's Day" (Revelation 1:10).

I have referred to my young days, when I kicked at being restricted in my activities, but I am sure my parents were right in putting the matter to me in this way. Because the Lord Jesus rose from the dead on Sunday, we keep this one day differently from the other six, to show our love for Him.

For me, it has not been exactly a day of rest, and I often call to mind the healing of the blind man in John 9. On that occasion, Jesus said: "I must work the works of Him that sent me, while it is day: the night cometh, when no man can work" (John 9:4). This, and most of His mighty works that are recorded, were performed on the sabbath. For Him, it was a day for saving men's lives, far removed from what was being taught — and cruelly enforced. It was this that led the Jews to seek His death. In this connection, He made His claims very clear: "I say unto you, that one greater than the sabbath is here . . . the Son of Man is Lord of the sabbath!" (Matthew 12:6-8).

On another occasion, He explained his behaviour in these amazing words: "My Father worketh hitherto, and I work" (John 5:17). It was this statement that was seized upon to put Him to death; following which, the next day being the sabbath, his body rested to await a new day — and what a day it was! Both for Him and for His disciples, before and after His ascension, it was a wonderful day for worship and witness.

The change of day was made necessary by the death and resurrection of Jesus. We read: ". . . and if any man be in Christ, he is a new creature: old things are passed away, all things are become new" (2 Corinthians 5:17).

"In Christ" is the condition of all who find salvation by placing their faith in the atoning death and resurrection of Jesus, and every true conversion will reveal a new behaviour pattern.

For me, in God's mercy, Sunday is still the Lord's Day, but I have thought of late that our freedom to use it for Him may soon come under attack. When I first wrote this

Under Instruction

in the summer of 1990, I could see Islam raising its head worldwide. But even since then there have been subtle and sinister pressures brought upon believers seeking to keep the day for the Lord. These things suggest to me that *the* "Day of the Lord" is very near.

My own Sunday School days were the time when my Christian experience got off to a good start because Bible texts were memorised, so that now at eighty-plus I can recall them, even though more recent events present a problem at times. Sunday School work has therefore been regarded as very important. The Sunday School at Harman's Cross dates back over fifty years, for many of which valuable help was given by Joan Hollister who, being of the same mind and also a teacher, took the work very seriously.

Today there appears to be a dearth of young Christians who are prepared in similar fashion to commit themselves to a work that lay close to the Saviour's heart, and so miss His joy in that respect.

13: Business As Usual

An outstanding event in my business life took place in April 1972, an added confirmation of the guiding hand of God at a time when I found it hard to keep up with the times. The truth was that neither I nor my staff wanted to change our ways, and I was giving serious thought to selling out — but always with some qualms about the way this would affect the staff, most of whom had worked nowhere else.

I had received a letter from my son-in-law, Stuart White, asking me to consider employing him as 'office boy' with a view to his taking over as manager when I retired. He was, at that time, reading Biology and working in an Epsom hospital. His elder brother had qualified but was facing problems finding work in that capacity.

My reaction to the letter was to take a train the following day for discussion. The result was that Stuart handed in his notice and put his house on the market. A month later he was in the office, taking the place of a girl who had left us.

Business As Usual

Again, the hand of the Lord was seen by me to be evident, in that both the office and the workshop staff accepted him, giving the help he needed for responsibility. They were no fools, and could see they had got someone who would give time to their problems. Both Stuart and I owe much to Peggy Burt and Brenda Chappell in this respect; also to Brenda's husband Ron, the Sales Manager. In little more than a year, the bookwork was updated. Stuart was a committed Christian, as was my daughter Jocelyn, and so, before many months had passed, a partnership was formed. For the first time, I was able to give my mind in a detached way to the problems of the customer.

It had been evident for years that the premises fell below the standards of those holding a Vauxhall franchise, and so in 1983 the site was cleared. The following year new offices, showrooms and stores were standing on the spot where, fifty years before, I was told my project would be a flop!

The bulldozer brought to light much that had been lost sight of for years and revealed a quality of workmanship that should have been followed: it was the work of Sydney Pearcey, to whom reference has been made. Perfectionists are not always easy to work with, but Sydney was the exception, so in no way was he discouraged in seeking the hand of my sister-in-law, Ruth Cleall. He died in 1976, and Ruth five years later, leaving Priscilla and three grandchildren, Ursula, Guy and Ralph. Many will think of him assisting G. K. Lowther in the building of the Gospel Hall in Roper's Lane, Wareham — both in its inception and planning and also in the services.

Unlike my daughters, globe-trotting was never my privilege — all my cash was locked up in the business and there was never any spare! So, apart from an unforgettable trip to Jersey in an old Dakota, and a much safer trip to Southern Ireland by car, all holidays were spent in these islands as a family; and what happy times they were, all

A SUNDIAL IN ANGEL SQUARE

The opening of the new showroom and stores, 1984.

on a shoe-string, thus enabling them each to have an education at Newton Manor School.

I have mentioned other members of my family, and I want now to speak of my dear Joan, who left us to be with her Lord on 2nd December, 1982, in her seventy-sixth year. It will be clear to the reader that her life was by no means an easy one. Severe asthma attacks often made things very hard for her, and matters came to a climax when she collapsed in the hospital when she went in for a check-up. She seemed well enough to walk in, but I arrived an hour later to find she had been put on a ventilator, and was told her condition was very serious. After three weeks we brought her home, and the Lord gave us nine weeks together, and happy weeks they were. I was able to give her all my time, we were able to read and pray and speak freely, both of us being fully aware that she would be unlikely to survive another attack.

I cannot forget that there had been occasions in the past when I would ring up from the garage to say I was bringing in someone to share the meal. Springing that sort of thing on her at short notice would be bound to affect her breathing — how could I have done it? I don't find it easy to write this, because too often I got my priorities wrong. Someone has said:

> Only one life, 'twil soon be past.
> Only what's done for Jesus will last.

That is very true, but some of us are dull, and need help in recognising duties that should take precedence. It is these He will recognise are done for Him.

Before Joan was called Home, and her breathing rather tight, she said, "I hoped I would be able to see Mildred married" — an event planned for nine months ahead (Mildred being the third of our four daughters). I silently recalled my sister saying before she died that she had hoped to look after Father until he was called Home. It was not to be.

All my daughters are believers, and I am unable adequately to express my joy in having a family that is completely united. Monica, my eldest, now retired from teaching, is happily married to Peter Perry and living in Budleigh Salterton. The next two are much further afield. After we lost our son David at four months, Winifred came next. She, too, entered the teaching profession. She married Roger Dow, of Hawaii, and that is where they are still happily established. Their three children, Carolyn, Sandra and Andrew have now left school. Mildred for a time worked in my office, but now she and her husband Michael Colliss live in Winnipeg, where they are very involved in their church. Jocelyn, my youngest, is right next door and, with her husband Stuart and myself, is a partner in Foley's. David, Steven and James make up their family, and they also foster Sonia.

So, like David who ends his Psalm as he begins it, "Bless the Lord, O my soul", I am with him when he says: "He hath not dealt with us after our sins; nor rewarded us according to our iniquities. For as the heaven is high above the earth, so great is His mercy toward them that fear Him" (Psalm 103:10-11).

Postscript

I have often been asked about my views concerning the state of the world, in the light of the fact that the gospel of Jesus Christ has been proclaimed for the past two thousand years.

Two world wars have shattered the hope of those who believed man was improving. The heart of man is unchanged, and remains so until the miracle of grace takes place, when he repents and seeks God's mercy.

Changes have been taking place in Europe with breathtaking speed, and I am glad to have my Bible to help me. We can easily be carried away into thinking that man has at last seen the light and, in effect, is saving himself. We have said elsewhere that man is in rebellion against his Creator, but God is in complete control of the situation. All that takes place in the world of men is by His permitted will. By Him kings reign, and some of these have been monsters! Before I refer to the last of these that will appear, I quote Paul's words to the people in Athens: "God ... commandeth all men everywhere to repent: Because He hath appointed the day, in which He will judge the world in righteousness by that Man whom He hath ordained: whereof He hath given assurance unto all men, in that He hath raised Him from the dead" (Acts 17:30-31).

This man is Jesus Christ. The Bible speaks of another man that is to enter the world's arena. This is what we read in Daniel about this man, or "king", as he is called (Paul refers to him as the "man of sin", 2 Thessalonians 2:3): "And the king shall do according to his will; and he shall exalt himself, and magnify himself above every god, and shall speak marvellous things against the God of gods, and shall prosper till the indignation be accomplished: for that that is determined shall be done" (Daniel 11:36).

Up-to-date reading, that! Maybe we can see pointers to

this coming anti-Christ, and his persecution of Christians. Their deliverance, and his destruction, will be effected by the coming of God's King. He will set up His Kingdom, and those who suffer with Him here will reign with Him there.

My understanding of the Bible in relation to present day happenings differs little from the teaching received in early days, when I realised that if I was to follow the example of Jesus I must make the Scriptures the starting point in my knowledge of God. At what age the Lord became conscious of his destiny we are not told, but Luke tells us that at twelve years he was making his Father's will for his life his first concern, and enlarges by saying that he was subject to his parents, "increasing in wisdom and stature, and in favour with God and man" (Luke 2:52), beautifully fitting words to cover the following eighteen years!

His submission to John's baptism in order to "fulfil all righteousness" marked his constant use of Scripture in his path of obedience. This path became increasingly clear when led by the Spirit into the wilderness to face Satan's suggestions for an easier pathway — and when, it should be noted, both made use of Scripture! Visiting his home town of Nazareth he was to meet the same "pick and choose" reaction to the truth as it was presented on that occasion. Later, facing the Jews in Jerusalem he said, "Search the Scriptures; for in them you think you have eternal life: and they are they which testify of me" (John 5:39). His healing on the Sabbath and his claim to be the Son of God, together with his use of their Scriptures, were fast leading him to the goal that lay ahead. It is, however, his words on the evening of his resurrection that give a lead to my understanding of those thirty years prior to stepping out into public life; they are as follows: "These are the words which I spoke to you, while I was yet with you, that all things must be fulfilled, which were written in the law of Moses, and in the prophets, and in the psalms concerning me" (Luke 24:44). For me, these

Postscript

words of the risen Christ to his disciples not only shed light on those "hidden years", but also on future events of trials and triumphs for the Church of God composed of Jewish and Gentile believers, now all "one in Christ", and also for Israel as a nation, at present "cast off" because of their rejection of the "Light", then restored in deep repentance. I find it important to enquire what Scriptures still await fulfilment, and surely the angel's message to Mary, Luke 1:30-33, is one such. As a boy I recall Father often prayed for the "peace of Jerusalem", no doubt with Psalm 122:6 in mind. He believed the conversion of Israel would not take place as a nation until the moment of Christ's return for His Church. I share that view, and though David doubtless had his son Solomon in mind when, guided by the Holy Spirit, he wrote Psalm 72, surely, as with many others in that collection, "a greater than Solomon is here"!

Getting back to present day happenings: no, I am not looking for the anti-Christ, but if and when he shows himself (and I am spared until that hour), I shall know that my Lord's coming is very near. When that takes place, some remarkable changes will occur to the faithful of every age. I, for one, am very conscious that I bear very little likeness to my Lord, but I have His word that He will alter all that! To Him be the glory.

But I cannot leave it there. Speaking of the Lord's return, the apostle John says: "And every man that hath this hope in him purifieth himself, even as He is pure" (1 John 3:3). This old disciple, who knew his Lord so well, had more to learn concerning God's holiness. On the Isle of Patmos, he was given a vision of his Lord that brought him down. He says, "I fell at His feet as dead." That which follows is precious. He says: "And He laid His right hand upon me, saying unto me, Fear not; I am the first and the last: I am He that liveth, and was dead; and, behold, I am alive for evermore, Amen; and have the keys of hell and of death" (Revelation 1:17-18).

* * * * *

In bringing this memoir to a close, on a personal note I want to thank my reader who is still with me. But I find myself wondering if the object has been achieved, because in using the word "Christian" as a starting point my intention was to describe my life's experience as a believer in a factual way without adding embroidery of any kind!

If this has been accomplished I would now urge any reader who is seriously concerned about his relationship with Almighty God to quit for ever self-reliance or self-effort, and to lean his whole weight on Jesus, the living Son of God, whose death and resurrection enable Him to pledge His willingness and power to be Saviour, Friend and Guide in response to that kind of acknowledgment of need.

My reader will have noted that being brought up in a Christian home is a privilege which increases responsibility but does not, in itself, save anyone. The key to this very important issue is a personal faith in the Lord Jesus that leads to repentance. This raises the question, "How shall we escape if we neglect so great salvation?" (Hebrews 2:3).

However, another possibility comes to mind — perhaps the reader has, like myself, experienced the new birth, but for reasons known to himself has become discouraged and has drifted back to a state of mind where all joy and assurance are gone; if so, I would earnestly suggest he read Psalm 51 for clear direction to restoration from despair. David had come this well-travelled road in repentance, a road I have myself come, a way back to a loving God who Himself planned it all; and it is with Him just here that I must leave my reader.

Postscript

* * * * *

THE SEEKER

I see the Light, I've found the Way;
My lot was night but now 'tis day.
For in my state of pride and doubt
A seeking God has found me out.

I sought no help from God's dear Son
Until I met that lovely One.
He came a long, long way for me
To seek me out and set me free.

Here was the Light, here was the Way
By which my night was turned to day.
When I, to Jesus, brought my sin
A loving God just took me in!

As "Father" now I speak to Him.
His Holy Spirit dwells within.
And, when ungrieved, He gives me song
Because to Him I now belong.

* * * * *